Working Green Wood
With PEG

Working Green Wood With PEG

Patrick Spielman

Sterling Publishing Co., Inc.   New York

Oak Tree Press Co., Ltd. London & Sydney

Acknowledgments

A very special thanks goes to my good friend, Harold Mitchell, of The Crane Creek Company. His generous assistance and advice about PEG over the years has deeply influenced this book. Much of his pioneering work with PEG has been of immense value not only to me, but to woodworkers throughout this country and abroad. It's been a privilege to be afforded the free and general use of his written and spoken words of wisdom about PEG which appear on these pages. A huge debt of gratitude is extended to the staff of Forest Products Laboratory (including those employees who have retired) for their cooperation and assistance, including George Englerth for his correspondence regarding his PEG experiences.

Also appreciated are the customers of Spielmans Wood Works who wrote or visited our shop to discuss problems, share solutions, and, in effect, help us to grow. The work of my former students must also be recognized, particularly that of Don Koepsel, Wayne Peterson, and Bob Kiehnau. Their projects, help, and enthusiasm were inspiring.

Thanks to Dr. Cote for his special contributions and to the following companies who have provided material and illustrations: The Crane Creek Co., Granberg Industries, Inc., Homelite, and Nalgene Ind. Products. Tender words of appreciation to my wife, Patricia, for her patience, support and special artistic talents in putting together our first booklet "Spielmans PEG Projects" of which this book is a greatly expanded version.

Contents

Photo Credits

Introduction

Illus. 1

Today, more and more people are rediscovering the value and importance of nature's most versatile and abundant provider—wood. High costs and shortages of energy account for the more than 25 million households in the United States that now use wood stoves and fireplaces for supplemental or primary heat. As we again turn directly to the forest for domestic fuel, a growing number of woodworkers are also finding that green wood is a low-cost and readily available project material.

Green, solid lumber is normally cured or seasoned (before woodworkers use it) by some means of air drying or commercial kiln drying. Over the years, these methods have, by and large, remained as the only accepted practices for preparing green wood to be crafted into fine woodwork. This is especially true for boards 1 to 2 inches (2.54 to 5.08 cm.) thick. Good-quality wood in thicker dimensions has never been readily available.

The best grades and even the most expensively processed woods do not come to the woodworker with a guarantee against cracking or checking, and conventionally dried or seasoned wood is still susceptible to swelling, shrinking, or cracking. These problems are caused by the uncontrollable changes in atmospheric moisture conditions in which the wood is stored, worked, and put into use or service.

This book is a basic handbook for woodworkers seeking an alternative, do-it-yourself method for curing their own green wood without degrade. The method employs a system using the chemical *polyethylene glycol 1000*—simply referred to as *PEG*. Essentially, the process involves mixing the chemical with water to form a solution for treating green wood by immersion. A proper treatment permanently restrains the green wood from swelling, shrinking, warping, or cracking, regardless of the atmospheric conditions to which it will be subjected. In effect, the wood is stabilized—"frozen," held forever in its green state.

The PEG process is ideally suited for projects such as solid-wood bowls, lamps, slab tables, and carvings—all of which require thicker materials and must remain crack free (Illus. 1). In projects of this type, the wood is worked "green." In fact, the greener the wood, the better the final product looks.

The process is a little more involved than simply dipping a chunk of wood into the PEG solution and expecting miraculous results. You must monitor the treatment. Yet, overall, the process is not difficult. This book will provide general guidelines in non-technical terms. The information is based upon authoritative data provided by the Forest Products Laboratory (Division, U.S. Department of Agriculture), the experiences of current leaders in the field, and my 20 years of experience. With the help of this book and the experience you will gain from working woods of your locality, you will achieve good results.

This book will also provide you with new ideas and an updated approach to working green wood with PEG. New products and recent developments are now available to small-scale home shop and school woodworkers that not only improve the process, but speed and simplify it as well. On pages 115-119, you will find a list of companies (with their addresses) where you can buy previously hard-to-get supplies and equipment.

Within this book, you will also find many drawings and photos of PEG-treated projects that will give you ideas for your own creative efforts. Since

Illus. 1 Projects crafted from PEG-treated green wood remain crack free and check free.

Introduction

you can obtain most of your green, raw wood free or for a low price, the major advantage of these projects is their low cost. True, if considered only on a per-pound basis, PEG is expensive. However, PEG is diluted with water and does not evaporate. Some of it is absorbed in the wood during treatment, but considering the amount of wood you can treat with a small amount of PEG, working green wood with PEG is an economical process for the woodworker who is able to obtain green wood.

Massive, solid-wood projects are unquestionably beautiful, and only with PEG can you make them with a truly defect-free, natural appearance. Now you can process your projects totally, every step of the way—you can cut your green wood from the tree and work it all the way to the finished project.

PATRICK SPIELMAN
Spielmans Wood Works

1

Wood–Its Structure and Moisture Problems

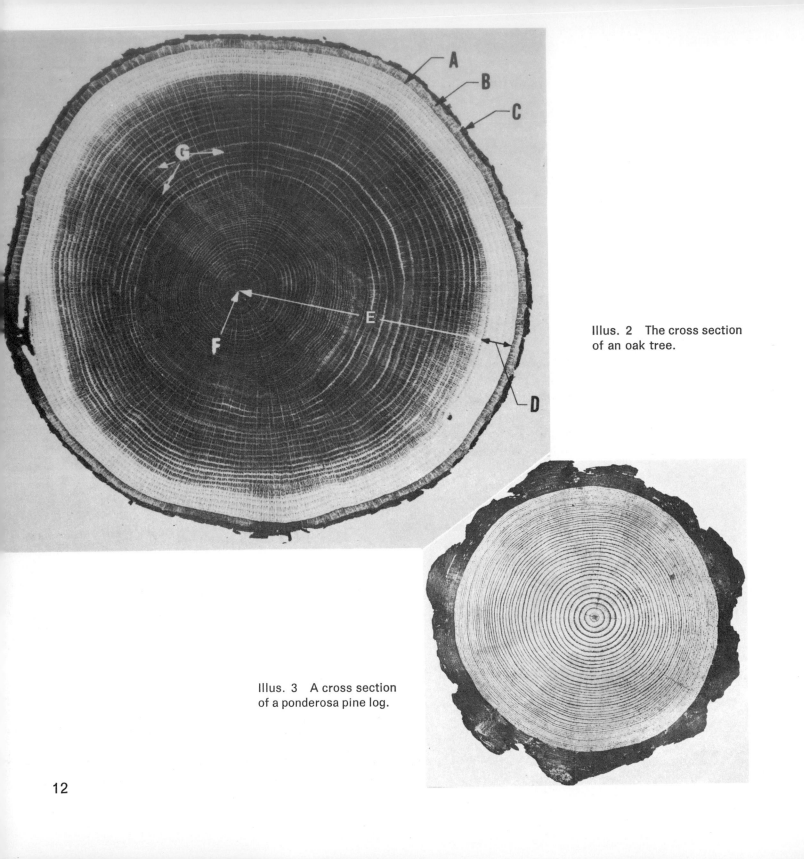

Illus. 2   The cross section of an oak tree.

Illus. 3   A cross section of a ponderosa pine log.

12

The cross section of a tree reveals the visible features of common woods (Illus. 2), including the well defined circular layers, called *annual growth rings*, which correspond to the yearly increase in growth. The *cambium layer* (Illus. 2, A) is made up of the newest growth cells, those that are produced each year, and is located between the bark and the sapwood. The bark consists of two layers—the *inner bark* (Illus. 2, B), which is the living portion, and the *outer bark* (Illus. 2, C), which is the dead corklike material.

The lighter-colored layers in Illustration 2 are made up of sapwood. In a living tree, the sapwood provides the channels for sap (or moisture) movement. The *heartwood* (Illus. 2, E) is the inactive part of the tree. In some species of wood, the heartwood can be more difficult to treat with PEG than the sapwood. Since the cells are dead, and absorb and lose moisture slowly, heartwoods are less permeable to liquids than sapwoods (Illus. 3).

The *pith* (Illus. 2, F) is the very center of the tree. It is often punky, and in some trees it is decayed. Hardwood has *wood rays* (Illus. 2, G), strips of cells that extend radially (from the bark toward the pith) within the tree. Their primary function is to store and to transport food. Although they are not always as visible as they are in Illustration 2, they play a major part in the checking and cracking that occurs during drying.

If we look at wood under a microscope, we see how much it looks like a sponge. The enlarged picture reveals thousands of hollow, tubelike cells (Illus. 4 and 5). These are formed from tiny cellulose fibers, which might be compared to hollow, double-ended toothpicks. However, they are drastically smaller than toothpicks. They are, in fact, only about 1/25-inch (1 mm.) long in hardwoods and about 1/7-inch

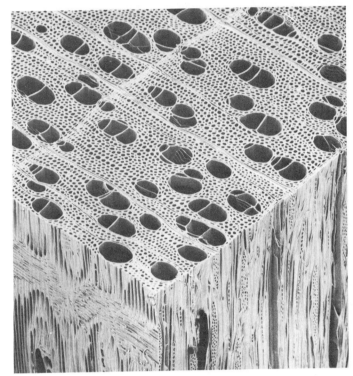

Illus. 4 The cellular structure of yellow birch, enlarged 100 times.

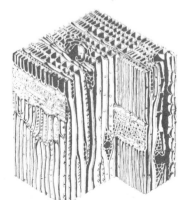

Illus. 5 A microscopic view of softwood shows its spongelike appearance.

13

(3.6 mm.) long in softwoods. Their diameters are as small as 7/1000 inch (.02 mm.), or the size of a hair. If we could remove one fiber at a time from just 1 cubic inch (16.4 cm.³) of wood, we would have about three million individual fibers.

There is no other material quite like wood, and no two species of wood are the same. For that matter, every *piece* of wood has its own distinctive properties.

Moisture content is the amount of water in wood. It is expressed as a percentage of the weight of oven (bone) dry wood. A live, growing tree contains a considerable amount of moisture, commonly called *sap*. Along with various amounts of other materials, sap consists primarily of water. Trees may range in moisture content from 30 percent to more than 200 percent of the weight of the wood substance, depending upon species and growth conditions.

Moisture in wood exists as *free water*, or water vapor in the cell cavities, and as *bound water* within the fine structure of the cell walls. Green wood is any wood in which the cell walls are saturated with water (Illus. 6). However, green wood often contains additional free water within the cell cavities. When all of the free water is removed and only the bound water in the cell walls remains, wood is said to be at its *fiber saturation point* (Illus. 6). Wood at this stage has a moisture content of about 30 percent. When the moisture content is lowered below the

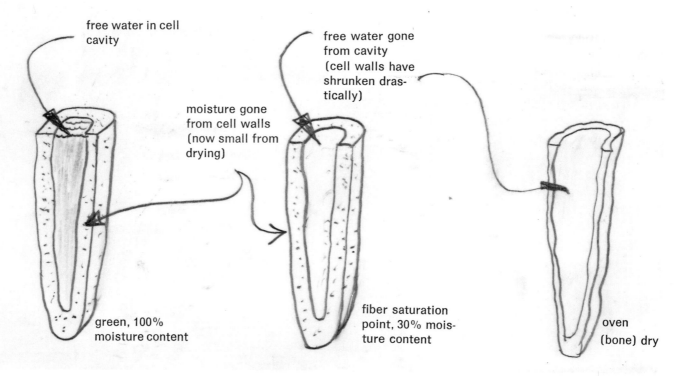

free water in cell cavity

moisture gone from cell walls (now small from drying)

free water gone from cavity (cell walls have shrunken drastically)

green, 100% moisture content

fiber saturation point, 30% moisture content

oven (bone) dry

Illus. 6 A quartered wood cell (fiber) at different stages—from green wood at left to oven dry at right.

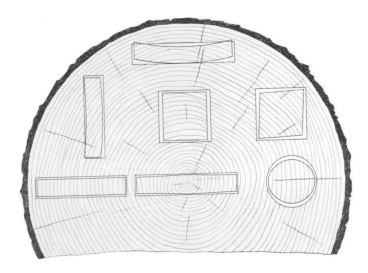

Illus. 7   How green wood can shrink and distort as it dries.

fiber saturation point, dimensional shrinkage begins to occur.

Wood is *hygroscopic.* This means that it will give off or take on moisture until the amount of moisture it contains is in balance with that in the surrounding atmosphere. Since wood loses and gains moisture from the air, it is subject to changes in humidity and temperature on a long-term (seasonal) and short-term (daily) basis. Wood attains *equilibrium moisture content* when it is neither gaining nor losing moisture.

Like sponges or other hygroscopic materials, such as salt, wood will shrink as it loses moisture and swell as it absorbs moisture. Wood shrinks when moisture is removed from the cell walls, but is dimensionally stable when the moisture content is equal to or above the fiber saturation point. As it shrinks and swells, wood warps, cracks, and splits.

Illustration 7 shows how the annual growth rings affect the way wood shrinks and is distorted. Wood does not shrink or swell uniformly or at the same rate in all directions. In a sawed board (Illus. 8), the amount of shrinkage is greatest in the direction of the annual growth rings (tangentially). A board shrinks only about half as much across the rings (radially), and only slightly along the grain (longitudinally). The combination of these different shrinkage rates sets up enormous stress within wood, causing distortion, warpage, cracking, and other drying defects.

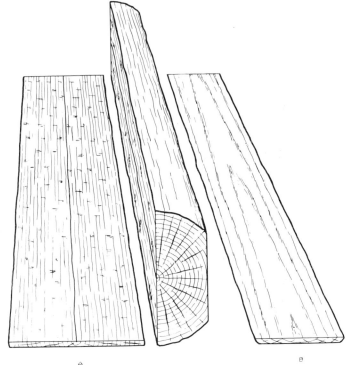

Illus. 8   Boards cut differently from the same log. A: Quarter-sawed—radial face; B: Plain-sawed—tangential face.

Most woodworkers insist that there is no substitute for dry wood. This may be true. But what happens when wood is not dried to correspond with the relative humidity of the environment in which it

Illus. 9   A steam-heated, ventilated, force air-conditioned, package-loaded dry kiln being loaded.

Illus. 10   In this do-it-yourself method of air drying, random-width boards are box-piled with air spaces between each layer.

will be used? It shrinks or swells and distorts from its originally worked configuration!

Kiln drying (Illus. 9) and air drying (Illus. 10) are the two conventional methods of drying wood. *Kiln drying* is a process in which lumber is dried in a closed chamber. Heat, relative humidity, and air circulation are carefully controlled until the wood reaches a predetermined moisture content. Obviously, due to the high costs of equipment, controls, and space, this process is not practical for a do-it-yourself setup. Most manufacturers of fine wood furniture and other quality indoor products use wood that has been dried to a uniform 6-percent moisture content. Many large companies have their own high-volume dry kilns. They also store the dried wood in air-conditioned, humidity-controlled rooms until it is worked into the final product.

Air drying (Illus. 10) is a relatively simple, do-it-yourself process. It is a good way to dry wood you

Illus. 11   This air-drying lumber pile is "roofed" with waterproofed building paper weighted down by low-grade boards.

will be using for outdoor projects. You can also condition air-dried wood for indoor use.

To air dry freshly sawed boards, stack them in layers with separating stickers so air can circulate through the pile and carry away the moisture (Illus. 10 and 11). As a general rule, air-dried lumber kept outside can seldom be dried below 12- to 15-percent moisture content. One-inch (2.54 cm.) thick, air-dried lumber, properly stacked outdoors in good drying weather for six months or more, will probably reach a moisture content of 18 to 20 percent. The chart on this page shows the approximate time it takes to air dry various woods 1-inch thick to 20 percent moisture content. It may take four times as long to dry 2-inch (5.08 cm.) thick wood.

The kiln-dried lumber you buy from your local lumberyard will not necessarily be free of shrinking and swelling problems. Few lumberyards store the material in humidity-controlled rooms or warehouses. Most use roofed storage sheds that often have open sides and dirt floors. Stored this way, kiln-dried wood is readily exposed to the surrounding humidity and

Drying Times

Approximate time to air-dry green 1-inch (2.54 cm.) lumber to 20-percent moisture content

Species	Time	Species	Time	Species	Time	Species	Time
Softwoods	*Days*	Sugar:		Beech, American	70–200	Sugar	50–200
Baldcypress	100–300	Light	15–90	Birch:		Oak:	
Douglas-fir:		Sinker	45–200	Paper	40–200	Northern red	70–200
Coast	20–200	Western white	15–150	Sweet	70–200	Northern white	80–250
Interior north	20–180	Redwood:		Yellow	70–200	Southern red	100–300
Interior south	10–100	Light	60–185	Butternut	60–200	Southern white	
Interior west	20–120	Sinker	200–365	Cherry, black	70–200	(chestnut)	120–320
Hemlock:		Spruce:		Cottonwood:		Pecan	60–200
Eastern	90–200	Engelmann	20–120	Black	60–150	Sweetgum:	
Western	60–200	Red	30–120	Eastern	50–150	Heartwood	70–300
Larch, western	60–120	Sitka	40–150	Elm:		Sapwood	60–200
Pine:		White	30–120	American	50–150	Sycamore,	
Eastern white	60–200	*Hardwoods*	*Days*	Rock	80–180	American	30–150
Jack	40–200	Alder, red	20–180	Hackberry	30–150	Tanoak	180–365
Lodgepole	15–150	Ash:		Hickory	60–200	Tupelo:	
Ponderosa	15–150	Black	60–200	Magnolia	40–150	Black	70–200
Red	40–200	Green	60–200	Maple:		Water	70–200
Southern:		White	60–200	Bigleaf	60–180	Walnut, black	70–200
Loblolly	30–150	Aspen:		Red	30–120	Willow, black	30–150
Longleaf	30–150	Bigtooth	50–150	Silver	30–120	Yellow-poplar	40–150
Shortleaf	30–150	Quaking	50–150				
Slash	30–150	Basswood	40–150				

From Forest Products Laboratory Publication No. 402

temperatures. It is likely to absorb moisture from the atmosphere, and, as a consequence, even the best of it will not perform much better than air-dried lumber. If you intend to use air-dried wood for indoor projects, condition it first. In a heated room where the air circulation is good, pile the wood in layers separated by 1-inch (2.54 cm.) stickers and let it dry out for another one to three months.

As you can see, you have to select green wood and dried lumber very carefully; the wood's intended use should dictate how it will be seasoned and conditioned. One-inch (2.54 cm.) air-dried or kiln-dried lumber will give you good results if you use the precautionary measures I mentioned. It is not practical to PEG-treat 1-inch-thick boards for furniture

and cabinet work unless you want a very high degree of dimensional stability, or you want to use a board to which the bark is firmly and permanently attached (bark eventually falls away as untreated wood shrinks).

PEG treatment is very practical for seasoning stock that is 1½ inches (3.81 cm.) or more thick. It is very expensive to kiln-dry lumber of this dimension, since the moisture content must be reduced to approximately 6 percent—the recommended amount for interior use. The purchase price of this lumber is accordingly very high, especially for quality kiln-dried material. Air-dried lumber of this dimension is likely to create problems during the drying process or later while in indoor service.

Illus. 12   The end checks in these thick boards are vivid examples of drying defects.

2

PEG–What It Is and What It Does

Illus. 13

In the mid-1950s, Dr. Alfred Stamm, a researcher specializing in wood-liquid relationships at the Forest Products Laboratory in Madison, Wisconsin, began the first-known work on the use of PEG as a wood-seasoning and dimension-stabilizing agent. Harold Mitchell, a fellow researcher at the lab, saw the tremendous potential of Stamm's experiments (Illus. 13) and joined him in researching and developing the PEG process. Stamm left the lab soon afterwards and funding was discontinued.

Fortunately, Mitchell was too interested and involved to quit. Using his own funding, he continued testing and experimenting in his own shop and laboratory and perfected the use of PEG. The Crane Creek Gun Stock Corp., then of Waseca, Minnesota, quickly realized the significance of Mitchell's efforts—the possibility of producing shrink-, swell-, and warp-proof rifle stocks (Illus. 14). Tests soon showed that rifles fitted with PEG-treated stocks consistently maintained higher accuracy. The stocks held up, whether they were used in the arid Southwest (where most ordinary stocks would shrink) or immersed in water for over a week.

Crane Creek provided some financial assistance for Mitchell's continuing research, and the Forest

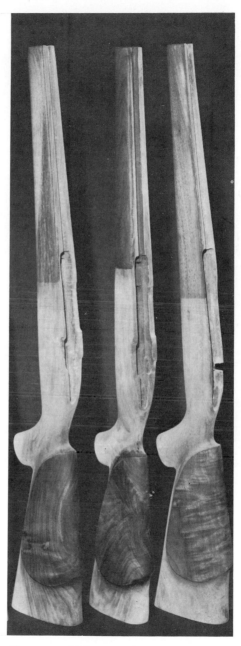

Illus. 14 PEG-treated wood was initially used to make rifle stocks.

Illus. 13 In one of his early experiments, Alfred Stamm treated sections of southern pine in a 30-percent PEG solution. The pieces were 11 inches in diameter and 1¼-inches thick and were all from the same log. The section on the upper left was untreated, the one on the upper right received an 8-hour soak, the one on the lower left a 16-hour soak, and the one on the lower right a 48-hour soak. After soaking, they were air-dried in an environment of 30-percent relative humidity.

Products Laboratory and the Forest Products Research Society published his major reports in their technical bulletins and journals (most of them appeared in the late '50s and early '60s). Crane Creek also supplied craftsmen with small quantities of PEG, as well as PEG-related literature and instruction sheets.

In 1972, Mitchell retired from the laboratory and purchased full control of Crane Creek Gun Stock Corp. He shortened the name to The Crane Creek Company, moved it to Madison, Wisconsin, and continued to supply PEG in small quantities. PEG is now available through a growing number of woodworking-supply companies. See page 115 for a listing of suppliers.

Polyethylene glycols are water-soluble chemical polymers ranging in molecular weight from 200 to 20,000. Physically, at room temperature the polyethylene glycols range from liquids to solids. The lower molecular weights, up to PEG-600, are liquid, water-white, hygroscopic, and water-soluble.

PEG-1000, of major concern as a wood-stabilizing and seasoning agent, is a waxy-white, semisolid, very hygroscopic material appearing much like paraffin wax. PEG-4000 and PEG-6000 are hard, waxy solids, usually available in flake form. These are not very hygroscopic, but are slowly soluble in water.

ADVANTAGES

Some of the most important properties of PEG are:

1 It is *low in toxicity*[1]. PEG would have to be consumed orally to produce injury. Skin and eye contact with PEG produces no serious irritations or sensations, and studies have shown that PEG is not absorbed through the skin. This is why polyethylene glycols are widely used in cosmetic creams, lotions, deodorants, suntan lotions, and the like. According to one study, rats that were test-fed PEG as 15 percent of their total diet revealed no adverse side effects.

2 PEG is a very *slow evaporator* so it does not pose an inhalation hazard and is not "lost" to the atmosphere.

3 PEG is *nonflammable*. It has a fire point of 580 degrees F. (304 degrees C.) so in itself presents no fire hazard.

4 PEG is *soluble in water*. It is easily removed from clothing and skin, allowing for easy cleanup of spills and drippings.

Stamm's early stabilization experiments included work with PEG of several molecular weights, but the PEG-1000 proved to be most satisfactory. When exposed to common atmospheres of lower relative humidities, unfinished wood treated with PEG of lower molecular weights had damp surfaces. Conversely, experiments with PEG of 1000 molecular weight only indicated surface dampness when the relative humidity exceeded 90 percent.

PEG should not be confused with ethylene glycol (a monomer) or with other polyethylene glycol polymers with greatly different properties. PEG-1000 has very special and unique properties for treating green wood and cannot be substituted by other related substances.

PEG-1000 is purchased as a room temperature solid. It melts at 104 degrees F. (40 degrees C.). It stabilizes the green or partially green wood, entering

---

[1]*Caution*: Personal safety should always be observed. The results from animal testing can only be used to indicate what effects might be expected to happen to humans. PEG is, after all, a chemical and should be dealt with prudently. Unusually high degrees of exposure to PEG (or, for that matter, to any kind of chemical), is likely to have serious physical consequences.

the fine cellular structure by diffusion. Its large molecules displace the natural moisture in the microscopic, latticelike structure of the fiber walls. For maximum dimensional stability, PEG must be diffused into the wood in amounts of 25 to 30 percent of the dry weight of the wood. Lighter treatments are satisfactory if you are using PEG as a drying or seasoning agent to prevent or minimize such defects as checking, cracking, and bark separation. In cases like this, your objective is to place only enough PEG into the outer shell of the pre-shaped object to adequately prevent drying defects that occur during humidity changes.

The density, structure, moisture content, thickness, and other qualities of each kind of wood have a bearing upon the treatment period. Woods that are low in moisture content are less effectively treated than green woods that are at or above the fiber saturation point. Consequently, partially dried wood should be soaked in water for two to three weeks before treating in the PEG solution.

You need very little equipment to get started with PEG, and you can reuse the PEG solution indefinitely by replenishing the small amounts of PEG the wood takes up in each treatment.

Green and partially dry wood is relatively easy to obtain. Since PEG-treated wood is highly stabilized, it is extremely predictable; you don't have to make allowances for expansion and shrinkage, and the bark of PEG-treated wood will remain attached permanently (Illus. 15).

PEG-treated wood cuts easier and faster, does not dull tools as quickly, and is much cleaner to use than other woods. You can cut, turn, and sand green wood without stirring up a great deal of dust.

The PEG treatment is fast. It's obviously not as fast as going to the lumberyard and buying a chunk of wood, but PEG provides the quickest way to

Illus. 15 Natural, bark-attached projects, such as this lamp, give the woodworker extra design options.

season your own green wood for predictable indoor use. You can heat the PEG solution (up to 140 degrees F. [60 degrees C.] for most species). In fact, some low-density woods, 1- to 1½-inches (2.54 to 3.81 cm.) thick, can be treated in 24 hours or less this way. Last but not least, PEG treatment is permanent (Illus. 16).

PEG does have some disadvantages, but they are minimal and easy to overcome. Surfaces that have been heavily treated with PEG can be somewhat difficult to sand by conventional techniques. In atmospheres above 90 percent relative humidity, unfinished PEG-treated surfaces become waxy and moist to the touch. Many of the conventional finishes do not work with PEG-treated wood, although there are a number of special and effective finishes available.

PEG treatment does not work on all species of wood. You cannot, for instance, effectively treat heavier and more dense woods, such as the heartwoods of maple and white oak. However, after all is considered, the PEG process scores highly on the plus side. If you are attracted to the jewellike, flowing, natural grains that only solid wood affords, and if you want that appearance to last, PEG is the process for you.

Illus. 17   This beautiful piece of untreated wood is "lost" as internal stresses give way to changes in atmospheric moisture.

Illus. 18   Notice the undisturbed, natural-flowing grain swirls of this one-piece, PEG-treated bowl.

Illus. 16   This slab of 1½-inch-thick end-grain oak, treated 20 years ago, has survived many drastic changes in atmospheric moisture.

Illus. 19   The glue lines in this laminated bowl quickly distinguish it as amateur woodworking.

3

Obtaining, Cutting and Storing Green Wood

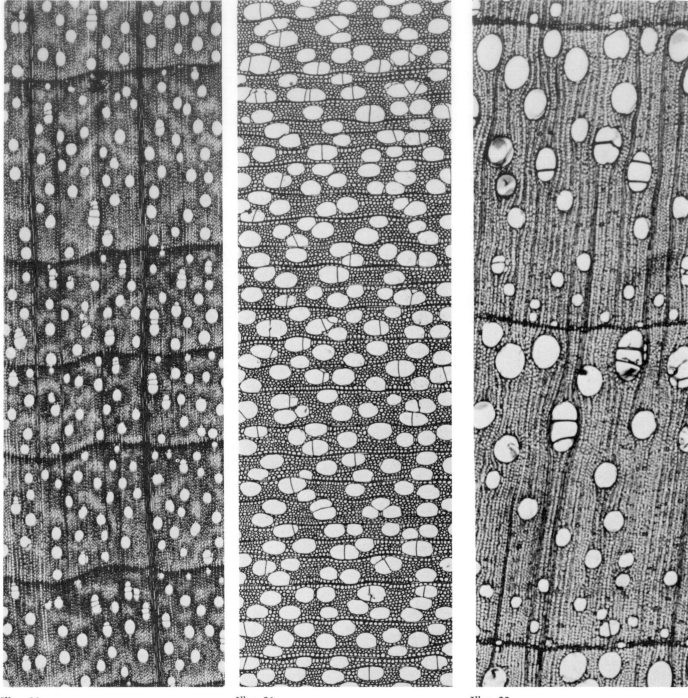

Illus. 20

Illus. 21

Illus. 22

There are over 500 million acres of forest lands in the United States; that's approximately two acres of forest, full of green wood, for every man, woman, and child in the country. Green wood is easier to obtain than you might think!

Anyone who prunes trees can supply you with green wood. You should also check with tree surgeons, city and county highway crews, utility companies (which cut trees to keep their lines clear), landscaping services, and park systems. Saw mills can often supply you with slabs, edgings, and flitches. Nose around construction sites. Even the firewood pile can be a good source of material for your projects. In forest regions, commercial logging operations are good contacts. Because their main prey is prime lumber, they often leave beautiful branches and stumps behind in the woods to decay. Check your local directory for listings under Excavating, Forestry, Landscaping, Logging, Lumber, Tree Removal, Trees, and the like. Call these leads and ask them what they have. Before you know it, you will have several sources for green wood—probably more than you will ever use.

If you accumulate a large supply of green wood, store it outside. On the north side of a building or in an area protected from the sun and prevailing drying winds, make a pile with the longest and largest chunks on the bottom.

THE TREATABILITY OF WOODS

Some woods are denser than others; that is, they have more wood substance than other woods of the same size or volume (Illus. 20–22). Every species has

Illus. 20-22   These cross-grain sections show woods of different densities (all are enlarged 20 times).

Illus. 23   This weed vase, made of splated birch, was turned, soaked in water, and lightly PEG-treated to prevent cracking.

unique microcellular characteristics, such as cell size and wall thickness. These structural differences account for differences in density. Low density woods, which are essentially the lightweight woods, are best suited for PEG treatment. With the heavier, denser woods, the diffusion of the PEG into the fine, cellular structure takes longer than it does in those woods with more spaces or larger cells.

Heavy, tropical woods are the hardest to treat, because of their extremely tight cell structures. Extremely dense native woods, such as osage orange and most of our desert shrubs, are also difficult. Although northern hard maple is only modestly denser than the average American hardwood, its heartwood is impossible to treat. No one knows why. White oaks are impervious to liquids (that's why they're used to make liquor kegs), so don't waste your time treating it. Red oak, yellow birch, beech, southern hardwoods, apple wood, and Douglas fir are treatable, but since they are all heavy and dense, they are more difficult to treat than other woods.

Softwoods, such as white pine, cottonwood, redwood, spruce, aspen, soft maple, willow, and butternut, are easier to treat than hardwoods. Splated wood (Illus. 23), which is heavily stained and on the verge of decay, can also be treated with PEG. After working this wood into its rough shape, soak it in water for a few days before putting it in the PEG solution.

CUTTING GREEN CHUNKS OF WOOD

Fast-cutting handsaws (Illus. 24), such as swede saws, bucksaws, or the one- or two-man crosscut saws, are suitable for nonpowered cutting. Today, most everyone who seriously works with green wood uses gas or electric chain saws. Take a good look at the chain saw safety precautions on page 29. A sawbuck is almost a must for cross-grain cutting (Illus. 25) and for lengthwise sawing.

Illus. 24   Most hardware stores have a good selection of handsaws for cutting green wood.

Illus. 25   Cutting a branch bolt for a lamp project.

Since you work them on a flat surface, green-wood slabs are the easiest materials to use. *Parallel slabs* are taken lengthwise from the log by cutting parallel to the pith (center of the tree). These can have a *tangential* or a *radial* face grain (Illus. 26 and 27, B and C). You can cut parallel-grain slabs with a chain saw, band saw, or handsaw. Because it is difficult to saw the slabs uniformly, allow for extra thickness. If you are sawing freehand, remember that the saw tends to follow the grain and sway off the intended path. If you are using a chain saw, there are several attachments on the market that work very well for sawing thick, parallel slab planks from logs (Illus. 28, 29, and 30). After you cut the slabs to the rough thickness, you can true and size them with a hand plane or jointer and surfacer.

Precautions to take when operating your chain saw

Remember, any powered cutting tool can be dangerous if it is not handled properly. It is always improper handling that causes accidents. Follow these precautions:

■ Always hold the saw with both hands, making sure that your thumbs are hooked around the handles —that your grip is tight. This keeps the saw from jumping if the teeth should grab accidentally.

■ Be careful not to let the end of the blade hit branches, stubs, stumps, or any other object than that which you are cutting.

■ Be sure that any helpers or spectators are at a safe distance from you and the saw, and that they are not standing where they might be struck by falling branches, etc.

■ Turn the saw off between cuts. Never hold it in one hand while you use the other to pick up cut pieces.

■ Don't carry the saw while the engine is running. Always turn the saw so the blade points backward when you walk with it from one cut to another.

■ Never use metal wedges or an axe to hold cuts open. Cut wooden wedges or pick up plastic wedges at your chain saw dealer's shop.

■ Never set the saw on the ground with the engine running. There is a chance that heat from the engine might cause fire.

■ Avoid refueling the saw in an area where spilled gasoline could soak flammable material. Never start the saw near the place where you refuel. Never refuel inside—not even in the garage. All of these conditions could produce a fire hazard.

■ When you are sharpening or adjusting the blade, wear gloves—or take extra precaution not to draw your finger across a sawtooth. Not only the sharpness of the teeth but also their shape makes them inflict cuts easily.

■ Always wear short sleeves or buttoned cuffs and generally close fitting clothes when you run your chain saw, to avoid the possibility that clothing might get caught in the saw.

Courtesy Homelite

29

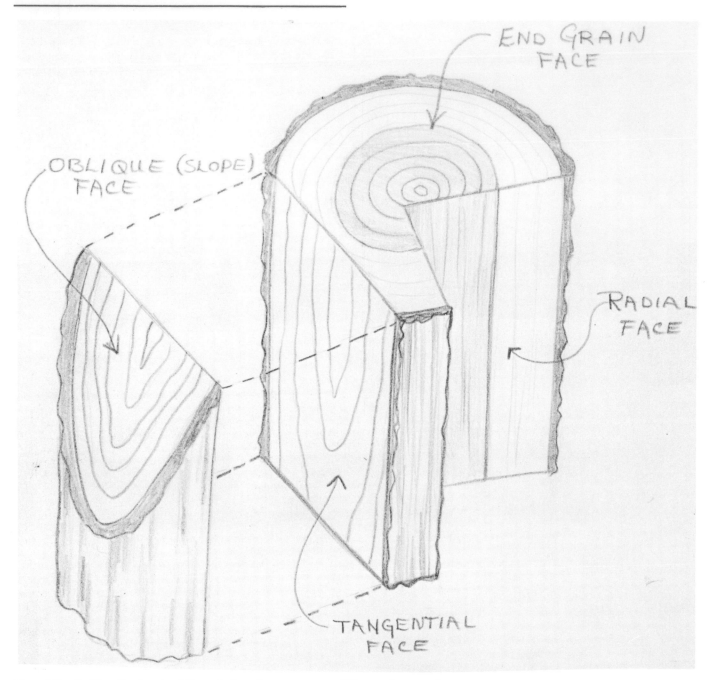

Illus. 26   Cutting the log in different directions exposes different face grains.

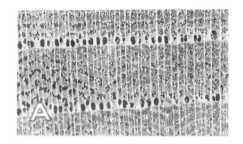 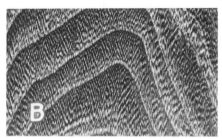 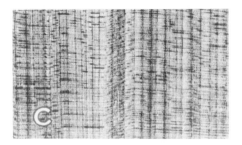

Illus. 27   The three faces of American elm. A: End grain; B: Tangential face; and C: Radial face.

Illus. 29

Illus. 28   A chain-saw attachment for vertical slab cutting.

Illus. 29   A chain-saw mill attachment will cut parallel slabs from large logs.

Illus. 30   A chain-saw mill in operation.

Illus. 30

Cut *cross-section slabs* (Illus. 31) at a 90-degree angle to the pith and have full end-grain faces. It is easy to cut cross-grain slabs, especially with a chain saw, but they are difficult to level, sand, and finish.

Oblique slabs are cut at an oblique angle to the center (pith) of the tree. Slabs of this type offer unique project possibilities, especially if you leave the bark on the wood (Illus. 32).

Be careful when you cut slabs on the band saw. The teeth can grab the slab and rotate it into the saw blade too quickly, causing it to bind, kink, and possibly break the blade (Illus. 33). Green wood can also pinch a saw blade. However, if you recognize the potential problems and take precautions, you can cut 14-inch (35.56 cm.) and bigger stock quite satisfactorily on most band saws. I recommend a coarse-tooth blade with plenty of set and large gullets to carry out the sawdust. You can also get good results with a ¾-inch (19 mm.) wide, three-tooth, skip-tooth-type blade.

Keep a strong grip on the wood when you make your cuts, especially at the beginning and at the end of the cut. With an extra-firm grip and a slow-enough feed rate, you should be able to keep the wood from spinning and make most cuts without difficulty. You

Illus. 31 Cutting a cross-sectional slab.

Illus. 32 This bark-attached slab makes an interesting clock.

can also support the stock so it will not spin. Illustration 34 shows one way to do this.

Level *rough-cut slabs* by hand or with portable power planes (Illus. 35 and 36) and power jointers (Illus. 37). You can also rig up your router to use for leveling (Illus. 38, 39, 40, 41, and 42). Use the widest flat-cutting router bit available. To achieve the cleanest cuts, feed the router in the direction against the rotation of the bit.

STORING GREEN WOOD

In order to keep your green wood from drying out, you must store it in an extremely humid place. The best way to store your wood for a long period is to immerse it in water, preferably in a plastic container. The surface water in the container will come alive with bacteria and mold growth; if you don't keep the wood submerged away from this mold, it will become stained. You can store wood this way indefinitely, although a strong stench may develop from the fermentation.

You can wrap the wood you are working on in plastic bags to keep the moisture from escaping (Illus. 43). However, even though it's wrapped in plastic, bacteria, mold, and fungi will eventually grow on the surfaces of the wood.

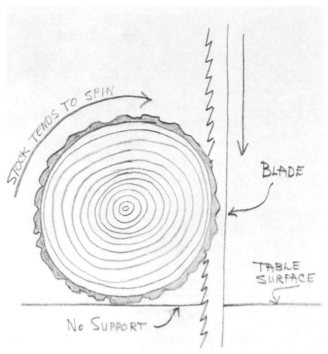

Illus. 33   The hazards of band-sawing round stock.

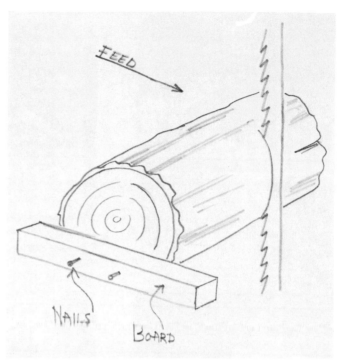

Illus. 34   One way of preventing round stock from spinning out of control during band-saw cutting.

Illus. 35   Leveling a rough-sawed slab with a hand plane.

Illus. 36   A portable, electric-powered plane makes quick work of sizing this massive table slab.

Illus. 37   You can level parallel and even oblique slabs with a power jointer.

Illus. 38 This simple system works well for leveling slabs with a router. The box frame keeps the router at constant height.

Illus. 39 This homemade device converts a drill press into an industrial-type overarm router—perfect for leveling slabs and many other industrial-type cutting jobs for the home shop.

Illus. 40 Slab leveling with an overarm router.

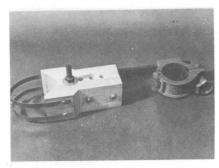

Illus. 41 The homemade overarm router jig.

Illus. 42 This commercially produced overarm router attachment features a good vertical depth-of-cut control.

Illus. 43 Slabs and bowl stock are kept green in plastic bags until ready for PEG vat treatment.

4

Vats for Treating

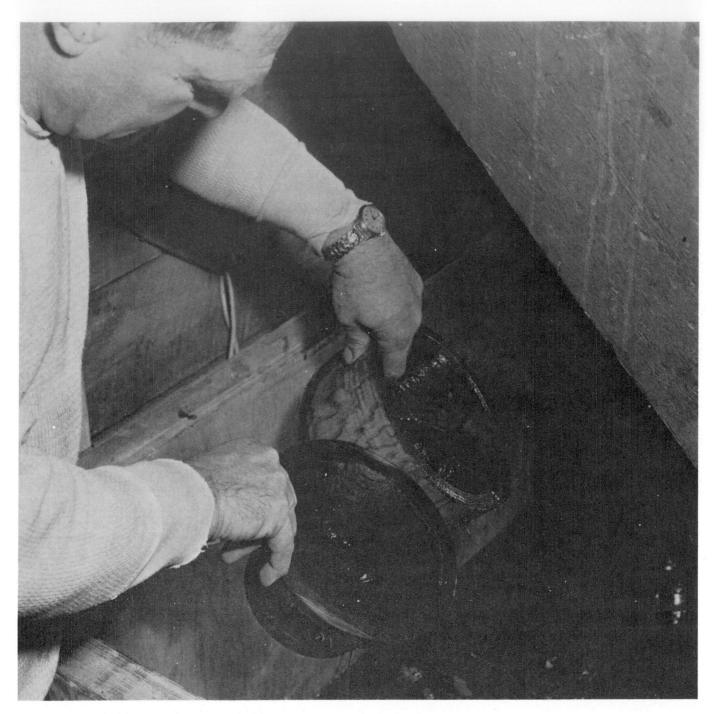

Illus. 44

When you begin working with PEG, use a cold (room temperature) solution and an inexpensive container as a treating vat. Select a container that suits your project; if you use a vat that is bigger than you need, you will waste chemical. Almost any container that will hold liquid will do, provided that it is made of nonferrous metal. When ferrous metals come in contact with the PEG solution, they react with the acid extractives of the wood to form iron oxide and cause the wood to darken and discolor. In fact, the wood will become so dark that you will not be able to distinguish the grain pattern.

After you've had some experience, you may want to speed up the process by using a heated system. However, if long treatment times are not an important factor to your operation, the cold system will give you good results.

MAKING A PLYWOOD VAT

You can make *plywood box vats* in any shape or size (Illus. 44 and 45). By installing portable (over the top) or permanent (through the side) heating elements, you can heat your unit to accelerate the treatment time.

Illustration 45 provides dimensions and construction details for a plywood vat. This size is appropriate for treating small pieces and medium-size slabs for tables. The primary disadvantage of a square or rectangular configuration is in its shape; much of the chemical is wasted because the solution fills the unusable corner spaces. You can fill the

Illus. 44 Removing rough-turned green-wood bowls from a homemade, plywood vat lined with fiberglass.

corners with rocks, but the deeper the solution, the higher you will have to build your rock piles.

Consider the overall costs before you build your vat. Add up the cost of materials, the waste, your own time, and the cost of hired help (if you are building a heated unit, you may need a licensed electrician for special wiring). In the long run, it may be cheaper to buy a commercially built vat.

If you still opt to build a plywood vat, be sure to use exterior-grade plywood. After cutting all the pieces, assemble them with marine-grade glue and use galvanized or aluminum finishing nails at the joints. If you are building a heated unit, you might want to insulate the cover. One way to make an insulated cover is shown in Illustration 45. You might also want to place rigid foam-insulation sheets under the vat, around the outside walls, and over the plywood lid. You can buy special mastics that make this job easier.

Your vat will look better if you cover the foam insulation with ¼-inch (6.35 mm.) plywood panels. If you hinge the cover, be sure to use solid brass hinges or continuous poly-hinges and brass screws.

You should line the inside surfaces with the kind of fiberglass used to cover wooden boats. This will assure you a completely leak-proof unit and will add considerable strength to the corner joints. I will provide some suggestions regarding resins and the fiberglassing procedure, but do not consider this information to be the complete or final word on the subject. It would be wise to check the library for a reference book about fiberglass work—especially if you have never worked with this material. Be sure to read all the instructions provided by your material manufacturers and suppliers. Here is a suggested procedure for fiberglassing your plywood vat:

1 Be certain that the inside corners are tight, clean, and smooth. Sand off any lumps of dried glue.

37

2   Make a fillet along the inside corners. This should be of a radius equal to that of your index finger. Use automotive body filler—the epoxy type is best. Any kind of wood filler will work, but if you use a water-mix type, be sure the moisture dries out completely before applying any of the fiberglass resin (polyester). Also be sure to fill and level any knotholes or voids in the plywood surfaces.

3   A word about resin: In general, 1 gallon of resin will cover about 45 square feet (4 m.²) of surface. Use a bonding-type resin for coating the raw plywood first. This remains somewhat tacky after cure, and forms a perfect bond between the wood and the successive layers of fiberglass. Mix no more than 1 quart of resin at one time. If you mix too much, it may harden before you get to use it. A gell-coat type of resin cures very hard and tack free. Use this for a final coating, covering all of the fiberglassed surfaces. You can also use it for recoating, but sand the surfaces first.

4   Begin the fiberglassing job by working the areas of the inside corners. Mix about 2 cups (480 ml.) of resin and saturate the plywood, working an area of 1½ to 2 inches (3.81 to 5.08 cm.) on each side of the corners. Allow the resin to soak in and cure. With this first application of resin, do not apply any fiberglass cloth. If you do, you may find that the resin will disappear into the wood and a poor initial bond

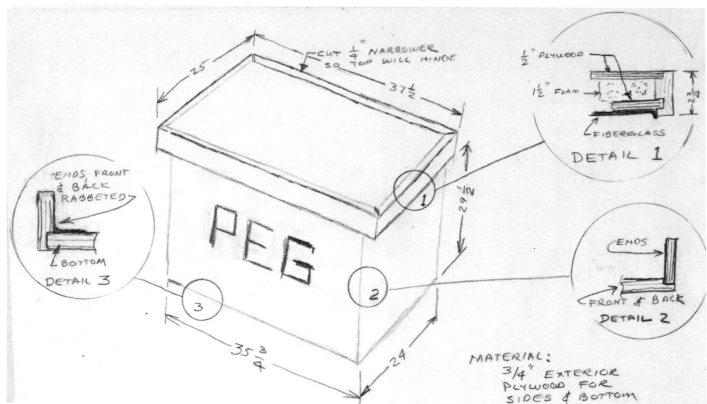

Illus. 45   Suggested construction details for making a **vat** for PEG treatment.

will result. Position the vat in such a way that you can work horizontally, one surface at a time. Give the plywood a good initial sealing coat of bonding resin (without applying the cloth), and allow it to cure. Apply resin to large surfaces with a mohair roller or pure bristle brush. Be sure to thoroughly saturate the end grains and plywood edges.

5   After the first resin coat has cured, lay cloth into the corners and apply another coat of resin. Use 9- or 10-ounce (255 or 283 g.) woven fiberglass cloth strip, about 2 to 3 inches (5.08 to 7.62 cm.) wide, to cover the corner areas. Fiberglass tape with woven edges is available in rolls for this type of work,

6   Spread the bonding resin onto the corner areas over the first coat of cured resin. Press the fiberglass tightly into the corners. Be sure to use enough resin to saturate the cloth thoroughly. The cloth will "disappear" if you do this properly. If white spots show up after curing, cut them open and feather out the area by sanding. Lay on a patch of cloth and more resin.

7   Cover the larger inside flat surfaces with 10-ounce (283 g.) cloth. Cut the fiberglass into separate panels, one for each surface. The cloth should be big enough to overlap the material you applied at the corners, but it should not extend around the corners onto the adjacent surfaces.

8   Work the large surfaces, one at a time, thoroughly saturating the cloth with resin.

9   Finally, after you have applied the bonding resin, coat all of the surfaces with the gell-type resin. You can sand sharp drippings, runs, or pointed fibers smooth after this resin cures.

TEMPORARY OR IMPROVISED COLD VATS

You can devise vats cheaply and easily. Plastic garbage containers (Illus. 46) and plastic pails (Illus. 47) make ideal cold-treatment vats and are

Illus. 46   This plastic trash container makes an ideal temporary vat for cold PEG solutions.

Illus. 47   Glass or plastic housewares, such as this pail, make good vats for small work. The stick wedged against the sides keeps the pieces completely submerged.

very inexpensive. They are especially good for small slabs, large bowls, and lamp bases. You will need less chemical if you use a round container, since there will be no unused corners in which solution goes to waste.

You can make *one-shot vats* (Illus. 48) to treat larger slabs, which you'll be using to make tabletops and large slab clocks. A simple wood frame supports

Illus. 48   This "one-shot" vat, for treating slabs, is made from a wood frame and sheet plastic. The slab is placed on sticks so the PEG will flow under it. The rock keeps the slab submerged.

heavy sheet plastic. Fill in the corners, as well as irregularities under the plastic, with sand, sawdust, or rocks. This way you'll need only a minimal amount of PEG to submerge the work.

Raise the slabs off the bottom with a couple of narrow sticks. This allows the PEG to flow under the work, insuring uniform penetration. Use a weight, preferably a heavy, nonporous stone, to keep the wood submerged; this will counteract its buoyancy.

Cross-section slabs, even as large as 5 feet in diameter, have been successfully treated in this type of one-shot vat. You can also use a child's plastic swimming pool, plastic tubs, and similar items; just be sure they don't leak. Loss of the chemical through a leak is not only messy, but expensive, too.

Commercially produced vats are available in 30-gallon and 50-gallon (114 l. and 209 l.) sizes (Illus. 53 and 54). They are made of industrial-quality plastic, are of durable-wall construction, and come with or without a heating element. When you order a unit with a heating element, you also get a lid and a perforated fiberglass element protector. Insulating floats are also available. The 50-gallon size is about half full when 100 pounds (45 k.) of PEG are mixed at a 50-percent solution; the 30-gallon size is about half full when 50 pounds of PEG are mixed in a 30-percent solution.

Mold, bacteria, or fungi will eventually develop on the surface of uncirculated solutions. Don't be alarmed. This is common, and you can skim off the growth periodically. Some woodworkers say they can eliminate this problem by adding a 1- to 2-percent concentration of borax (cleanser) or sodium penta-chloro-phenolate to the PEG solution. However, I've had only moderate success with these additives.

HEATING ELEMENTS

Many woodworkers install the type of *heating elements* used in household hot-water heaters in their plywood vats. As long as they are always kept completely submerged, brass or copper fittings will not contaminate the solution. Obviously, stainless steel is the best material for elements and fittings.

Be sure to check out all related expenses before purchasing an element. Some heating elements require heavy-duty wiring and separate control units for temperature regulation. A 1,500-watt element will

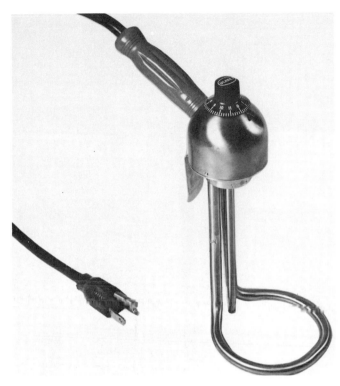

Illus. 49   This 1500-watt, 110-115 V. unit will handle most plywood vats.

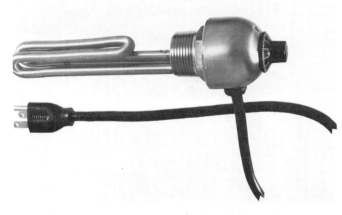

Illus. 50   This 500-watt portable element is ideal for heating solutions in temporary vats.

Illus. 51   The portable element in use.

handle most requirements in vats up to 36 cubic feet (1.1 m.³). This will heat about 1,000 pounds (450 k.) of solution (250 pounds [112.5 k.] of PEG and 750 pounds [337.5 k.] of water for a 30-percent concentration), and will occupy about 14 cubic feet (.42 m.²), or less than half of the vat capacity.

You can buy a compact, stainless-steel unit (Illus. 49) with an integral thermostat mounted on the end of the element unit. This unit is inserted through the side of the vat. Since it operates on 110-115V current, it requires no special wiring. A portable unit of a similar type is also available. This smaller unit works well in temporary or "one-shot" vats (Illus. 50 and 51).

Here are some tips for the use and care of heating elements:

1 All heating elements must always be fully immersed during operation to prevent burn-out.

2 When using portable elements, always be sure that the recommended length of the element is immersed to the proper distance.

41

Illus. 52   This element protector is made of perforated fiberglass.

3 Always have an extra margin of solution depth over the element. During long heating periods at high temperatures, the solution level may drop due to evaporation of water. Water will evaporate at a surprisingly fast rate even in covered, but not airtight, vats.

4 Install a through-the-side-type element close to the bottom of the vat. It should not, however, touch the bottom or the sides. Protect it from jarring or bending; be especially careful when you are immersing the wood. You can protect the element with some type of perforated fiberglass channel, such as the one in Illustration 52, or you can pile stones around it. Do not pile stones so close together that they close off the element's contact with the solution.

5 Periodically remove the mineral scale that forms on the surfaces of the heating element, since scale causes the element to burn out prematurely. Never use limestone or other sedimentary calcium-carbonate type rocks in the vat; these rocks promote scale growth.

6 Periodically remove sawdust, bark chips, and other sediment from the bottom of the vat.

7 The outer shell of the element, the part on the outside of vat that contains connections or temperature-control dials, usually is not waterproof. If moisture (or chemical) enters this area, it can corrode the contacts. So, when you fill the vat, add solution, or remove the treated wood, be careful not to spill liquid on the part of the element outside the vat.

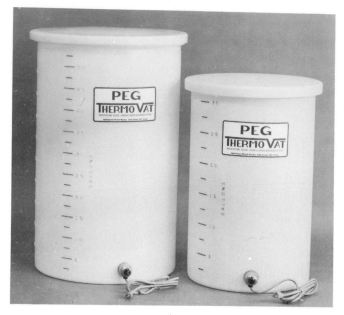

Illus. 53   The Thermo Vat is designed for heating PEG solutions. The 30- and the 50-gallon sizes are pictured.

Illus. 54   A small Thermo Vat in use.

5

Mixing PEG Solutions

Illus. 55   PEG is solid until it is dissolved in warm water.

Woodworkers commonly use solutions that are 30 and 50 percent PEG by weight. The table of standard PEG solutions on page 46 gives the PEG-to-water ratios required to make various quantities of mixed solution.

To estimate the amount of PEG you will need for a one-shot job, place the object to be treated in the smallest possible container and pour in a pre-measured volume of water to cover it. Check the table to see how much PEG you need. Remember, you can fill in voids or empty spaces, such as the insides of bowls, with nonporous rocks or stones. This will raise the level of the solution, but reduce the amount of PEG you need.

It may take several days to dissolve the PEG into the required amount of cold tap water. You can speed up the process by breaking the solid PEG into smaller pieces (Illus. 55). Use warm (or hot) water and stir until the PEG is thoroughly dissolved. You can also melt the PEG in a separate, nonmetallic container, then pour it into the water. Remember, PEG melts at 104 degrees F. (40 degrees C.).

A 30-percent solution of PEG has a specific gravity of 1.05 at 60 degrees F. (16 degrees C.). A 50-percent solution has a specific gravity of 1.093 at 60 degrees F. To test a new or used solution of PEG for the proper concentration, cool a small sample to 60 degrees F. in the refrigerator, pour it into a suitable container, and check it with the hydrometer (Illus. 56). Be sure the hydrometer floats freely. Read the scale at the liquid level. It is not necessary to maintain a high degree of accuracy with the optimum specific gravity. However, it is best to try to stay within a range of plus or minus 10 percent.

Water will evaporate during the long treatments, even when you are using covered, but not air-tight, vats. You can adjust for this, of course, by adding more water to the solution. Even better, you can drastically reduce evaporation by using expanded polyethylene covers or interlocking Mini-Vaps® (Illus. 57). Mini-Vaps also retard heat loss and can be used in vats heated up to 140 degrees F. (60 degrees C.).

PEG does not volitalize or evaporate from the solution even at high temperatures. However, water will evaporate from your heated solution, and you will have to add more from time to time.

Illus. 56 Test a sample of the PEG solution cooled to 60 degrees F. for the proper specific gravity with a hydrometer.

Illus. 57 These floating, interlocking vapor retarders help reduce water evaporation from the PEG solution.

Chapter 5

How to Make 30-Percent PEG Solution

Weight of Solid PEG		Dissolved in following amounts of tap water[1]				Will make following amounts of 30 percent solution[2]	
Pounds	(kg.)	Pounds	(kg.)	Quarts[1]	(l.)	Quarts[1]	(l.)
4.46	(2.0)	10.43	(4.7)	5.0	(4.7)	7.0	(6.6)
10.00	(4.5)	23.33	(10.5)	11.2	(10.5)	15.4	(14.6)
20.00	(9.0)	46.66	(21.0)	22.4	(21.0)	30.8	(29.2)
30.00	(13.5)	69.99	(31.5)	33.6	(31.5)	46.2	(43.9)
40.00	(18.0)	93.32	(42.0)	44.8	(42.0)	61.6	(58.5)
50.00	(22.5)	116.65	(53.0)	56.0	(53.0)	77.0	(73.1)

[1] At 60° F.

[2] A 30 percent (by weight) PEG solution, at 60° F., has a specific gravity of 1.05, contains 2.6 pounds of PEG per gallon, and weighs 8.65 pounds per gallon.

How to Make 50-Percent PEG Solution

Weight of Solid PEG		Dissolved in following amounts of tap water[1]				Will make following amounts of 50 percent solution[2]	
Pounds	(kg.)	Pounds	(kg.)	Quarts[1]	(l.)	Quarts[1]	(l.)
10	(4.5)	10	(4.5)	4.8	(4.5)	8.48	(8.0)
20	(9.0)	20	(9.0)	9.6	(9.0)	16.96	(16.1)
30	(13.5)	30	(13.5)	14.4	(13.5)	25.44	(24.2)
40	(18.0)	40	(18.0)	19.2	(18.0)	33.92	(32.2)
50	(22.5)	50	(22.5)	24.0	(22.5)	42.40	(40.3)

[1] At 60° F.

[2] A 50 percent (by weight) PEG solution, at 60° F., has a specific gravity of 1.093, contains 4.717 pounds of PEG per gallon, and weighs 9.434 pounds per gallon.

Reprinted courtesy Crane Creek Company

6

Treating and Drying Green Wood

Illus. 58   These blocks of walnut were treated to preserve them for future use.

48

Although woodworkers don't normally treat bolts (sections of logs) to preserve them for future projects, you can treat sections that are 2- to 4-inches (5.08 to 10.16 cm.) thick and sections in which the end-grain faces are exposed. However, since a heated PEG solution will effectively penetrate only 2 inches of an end-grain section of walnut or other medium-density wood (Illus. 58), you couldn't treat a bolt any thicker than 4 inches (PEG will penetrate 2 inches on each side).

You'll have the most luck treating wood that is already in the shape and size of your project. Work of this type generally requires lighter treatments, depending, of course, on the total bulk size (thickness and grain length). Even a relatively light PEG treatment will protect the work against splitting and checking during drying and penetrate the wood enough to give you an adequate skin or shell.

Work your project to within ¼ to ½ inch (6.35 to 12.7 mm.) of its final size or shape. This allowance will enable you to clean up your project and work it to its final form after you treat and dry it. A ½- to 1-inch (12.7 to 25.4 mm.) PEG penetration is considered about average for side grains of woods having lower densities. Plan on less penetration with denser hardwoods. The type of grain exposed on the larger surfaces also influences PEG penetration; PEG will penetrate deeper and faster into end grains.

Treating Schedules

The soaking time you need to treat a project is contingent on a number of factors. The major considerations are the kind of wood (its density) and type of graining, the concentration of the solution, and the temperature of the solution. You can speed up the diffusion of the PEG into the wood and decrease the soaking time by using the more con-centrated (50 percent) PEG solution or by increasing the temperature.

Researchers at Forest Products Laboratory did most of their PEG tests with walnut, a medium-density wood. The treatment schedule on page 50 is based on their findings. You can use these figures to estimate the treatment times for woods that are lower and higher in density than walnut.

Soak cross sections of woods with lower densities, such as white pine, spruce, redwood, soft maple, cottonwood, willow, and butternut, for one-half or two-thirds as long as you would walnut. For yellow birch, beech, red oak, apple, and other high-density woods, double or triple the treating times.

You can elevate the temperatures to treat very dense woods and the burls of most species. Experiment with the wood from your own locality to determine the best treatment schedule. Growth conditions and wood densities vary. It will take you longer to treat southern hardwood, for example, than it will to treat hardwood grown in Michigan.

For some projects, you will have to treat the wood to eliminate drying effects *and* to stabilize it (to ensure that it will not swell or shrink in humid or dry environments). To obtain a high degree of dimensional stability, elevate the temperature of the solution and diffuse PEG into the wood until you get a minimum retention of 25 to 30 percent of the dry weight. With most wood you can obtain this level of penetration by using a solution no warmer than 140 degrees F. (60 degrees C.); never raise the temperature higher than that.

You will have to over-treat the outer surfaces in order to attain the desired PEG level in the center of the wood. For example, by the time the center of a 1¼-inch (3.2 m.) thick slab has taken up the desired amount (25 to 30 percent) of PEG, the outer surfaces will have taken up about 40 percent. Getting

Treatment Schedules for Walnut

Solution concentration and temperature	Suggested period of soak for walnut disks	
	Up to 9 inches (22.86 cm.) in diameter and 1- to 1½-inches (2.54 to 3.81 cm.) thick	More than 9 inches (22.86 cm.) in diameter and 2- to 3-inches (5.08 to 7.62 cm.) thick
	Days	Days
30 percent, 70°F. (22°C.)	20	60
50 percent, 70°F. (22°C.)	15	45
30 percent, 140°F. (60°C.)	7	30
50 percent, 140°F. (60°C.)	3	14

the PEG deeper and deeper into thick pieces of wood drastically increases the required treatment times. In general, it is very impractical to treat woods that are over 1¼-inches thick for a high degree of dimensional stability.

You may find some woods that will present special problems that you cannot resolve with a heavier concentration (50 percent) and elevated temperatures. Honeycombing is a condition marked by thin, diamond-shaped cracks or openings that develop below the surfaces (Illus. 59). In cherry, you can reduce, and often eliminate, the honeycombing condition by lowering the temperature to 110

degrees F. (43 degrees C.) and lengthening the treatment time by approximately one-third. As a general guideline, you can treat a 1-inch (2.54 m.) thick piece of cherry with a 50 percent solution at 110 degrees F. for 45 days. Heavier cherry turnings, as shown in Illustration 60, have also been effectively treated. However, before treatment, a ¾-inch (19 mm.) diameter hole was bored completely through the vertical center and many additional holes were drilled (upwards) from the bottom to allow greater PEG penetration into the project.

Fine checks or cracks may occasionally appear, despite your careful treatment. Sometimes these

Illus. 59   Internal separations like these are called honeycombed failure.

Illus. 60   This heavy cherry lamp was turned from a branch with an oval cross-sectional shape.

defects are in the green log or tree even before you put a hand to it, the results of wind damage and other stresses. Often they develop when you fell the tree.

In partially dry slabs or chunks of wood where the outer surfaces are below the fiber saturation point, internal stresses may already have been set up. In the early stages of treatment, these tensions are released in the form of checks and cracks. Partially dried woods treated with PEG may also be susceptible to warpage. This is due to the differences in the way green and partially dry woods absorb PEG as well as to internal tensions. If you think your piece

of wood might be below the fiber saturation point, soak it in water for two weeks or longer so the dry areas take on moisture.

Sometimes wood in a firewood pile will still be green and treatable. However, the ends will tend to check and crack. So, simply cut the ends off to expose the treatable green wood. If you think the wood might still be too dry for treatment, soak it in water for two to three weeks.

DRYING TREATED WOOD

After you remove the treated wood from the vat, take a water-moistened sponge and lightly wipe the surfaces to remove sediment or any scum. Do not wash the treated wood under a stream of tap water; this will cause the PEG, which is water soluble, to leach out.

The thickness of the wood, the temperature, and the relative humidity affect the amount of time it takes to dry PEG-treated projects.

You can air-dry the projects in a heated room, or, in many cases, even dry them in a kitchen oven. Don't air-dry treated wood out of doors; it will take considerably longer than it will indoors. Pile disks, slabs, and other flat, parallel pieces with stickers between each layer as shown in Illustration 61. Even large treated disks, 4-inches (10.16 cm.) thick by 40 inches (102 cm.) in diameter, will dry in six to eight weeks in a heated room. You can hang bowls, lamps, and carvings with string from beams and rafters. The air is warmer near the ceiling, and you get free air movement all around the objects.

On a commercial basis, PEG treatment has been found to reduce the drying time required in conventional dry kilns. At home, you can efficiently force-dry small, PEG-treated objects in a kitchen oven (Illus. 62). Low-density woods, such as cottonwood, willow, and butternut, will dry sufficiently in

51

six to eight hours at 180 degrees F. (82 degrees C.) (Illus. 63). Heavily treated walnut of about 1-inch thickness has been successfully dried in eight hours in a 220-degree F. (104 degree C.) kitchen oven. With properly treated wood, there will be no surface checking, end splitting, or warping, regardless of how fast the moisture is removed.

The objective of the drying process is to dry only the outer-surface shell to a depth of ¼ to ½ inch (6.35 to 12.7 mm.). It is not essential that the wood be completely or uniformly dry throughout its total thickness before you start the final-finish cutting and sanding.

Illus. 61

Illus. 62

Illus. 61   These slabs are air-drying in a heated room.

Illus. 62   You can dry your turnings in a kitchen oven.

Illus. 63   This slab and this bowl, both of butter-nut, were oven-dried (ready for final smoothing) in 6 hours at 180 degrees F.

7

Small Slab Projects

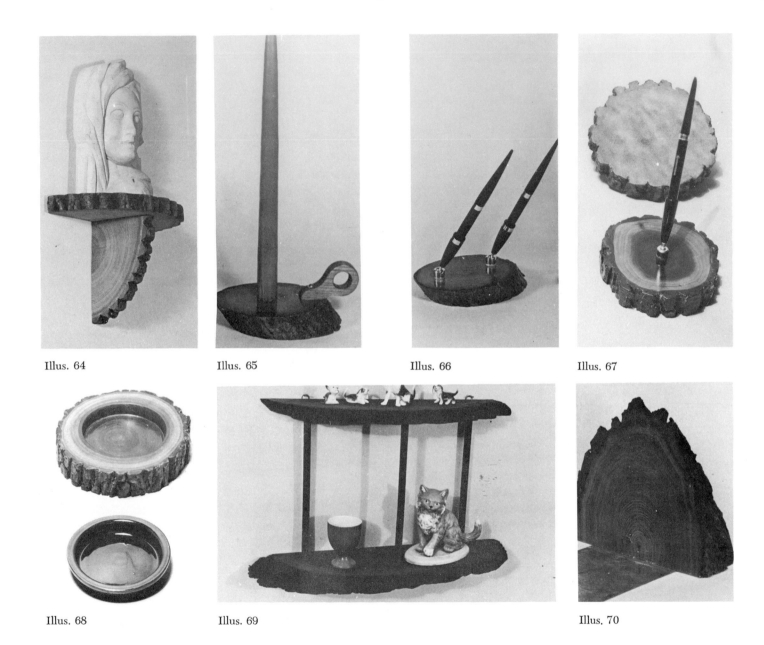

Illus. 64

Illus. 65

Illus. 66

Illus. 67

Illus. 68

Illus. 69

Illus. 70

Illus. 64-70 You can make all of these attractive—and useful—household objects from PEG-treated slabs and disks.

54

You can make shelves, bookends, candle holders, picture frames, and a number of other simple projects from cross-section disks and parallel and oblique-cut slabs. Obtain the hardware you need for these projects from the sources on pages 115–119.

The illustrations on page 54 give some ideas for pen sets, ashtrays, and candle holders. Illustration 70 shows a classic set of bookends made from the two halves of one oblique slab. Pieces of 20- or 22-gauge galvanized sheet steel are screwed to each slab and the bottoms are covered with a thin layer of felt to protect table surfaces.

Slabs also make interesting shelves. In fact, thick, parallel-cut slabs, with bark attached to the edges, make great fireplace mantels. Some other ideas for shelves are shown in Illustrations 71 and 72. Illustrations 73–76 will give you a few ideas on how to display family photographs on PEG-treated wood stands. See Illustrations 77–81 for candle holder projects and Illustrations 82–85 for lamp projects.

You can turn any kind of slab into a wall or mantel clock. Inexpensive, battery-operated, or standard-electric movements, with long stems made especially for craft projects, are easy to obtain (see pages 115–119). Use a slab that is at least 1½-inches (3.81 cm.) thick; thicker slabs are especially good for slick, contemporary designs (Illus. 86–90). The recess for the clockworks should be deep enough for you to bring the shank through to anchor and mount the hands.

To begin, mark the center of the clock on the front of the slab. Drill a small hole to the center of the back of the surface. Bore a large hole, or use a router, to make a recess for the clockworks. You can use brass nails, cast plastic or metal numbers, coins, buttons, rocks, shells, and many other objects as hour markers. Using a templet pattern like the one in Illustration 91 (you might want to transfer this to transparent paper), lay out the hour markers. Place the templet at the optimum position on the face of the clock, and, using a pointed tool, such as a scratch awl, punch through the paper templet to locate the hour markers on the wood.

Illus. 71

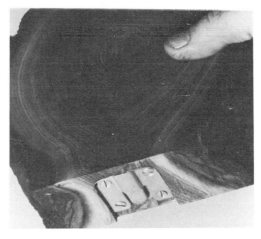

Illus. 72

Illus. 71-72 This unique shelf, made from a 2½- to 3-inch-thick slab, juts out from the wall. It is hung with a flush-mount interlocking wall hanger.

Illus. 73

Illus. 74

Illus. 75

Illus. 73-75 These photo mounts are easy to make.

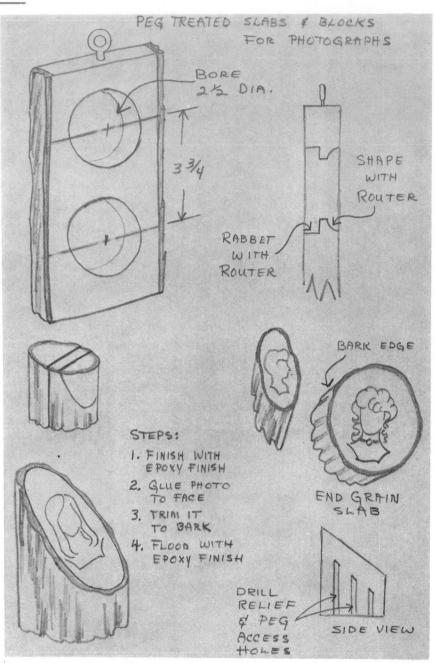

PEG TREATED SLABS & BLOCKS FOR PHOTOGRAPHS

BORE 2½ DIA.

3¾

SHAPE WITH ROUTER

RABBET WITH ROUTER

BARK EDGE

END GRAIN SLAB

STEPS:
1. FINISH WITH EPOXY FINISH
2. GLUE PHOTO TO FACE
3. TRIM IT TO BARK
4. FLOOD WITH EPOXY FINISH

DRILL RELIEF & PEG ACCESS HOLES

SIDE VIEW

Illus. 76 Details for making PEG-treated slabs and blocks to mount photographs.

Illus. 77

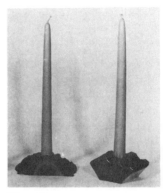

Illus. 79

Illus. 80

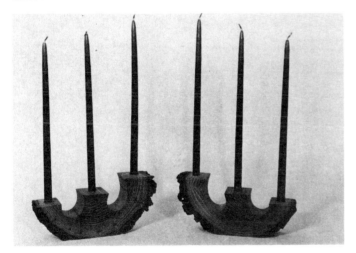

Illus. 78

Illus. 79   Even the smallest scraps of PEG-treated
disks can be made into
candle holders.

Illus. 80   A hurricane
lamp turned from a thick
disk; the glass chimney is
available at most hardware
stores.

Illus. 81   These candle
sconces were made from
a curved branch, split
lengthwise and flattened.
The holder brackets are
made from cross-sectional
disks.

Illus. 77   You can make
natural candle holders
from the crotch of a tree.

Illus. 78   This pair of
candle holders is made
from one cross-sectional
disk.

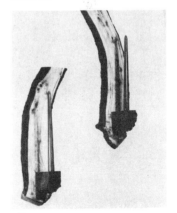

Illus. 81

57

Illus. 82

Illus. 83

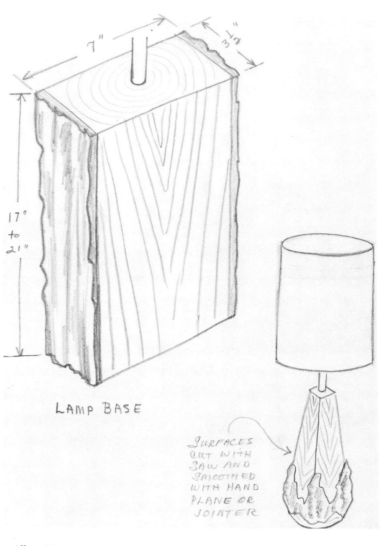

7"

3 1/2"

17"
to
21"

LAMP BASE

SURFACES
CUT WITH
SAW AND
SMOOTHED
WITH HAND
PLANE OR
JOINTER

Illus. 84

Illus. 85

Illus. 82   Oblique slabs are ideal for wall lamps.

Illus. 83   Halves of disks can be made into a matching pair of lamps.

Illus. 84   This lamp is made from a partially dried log, the bark of which has been removed.

Illus. 85   Flattened tree bolts serve nicely as lamp bases.

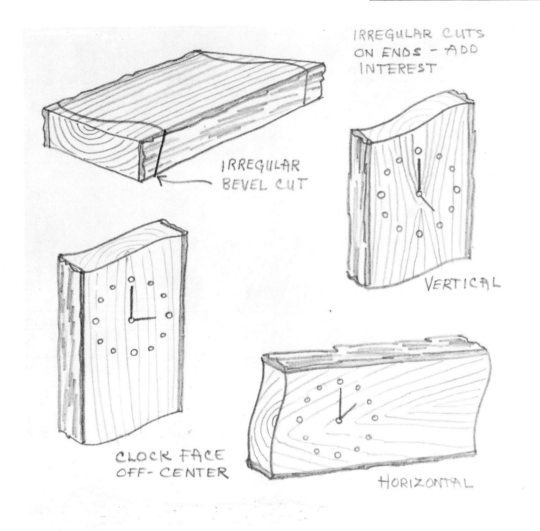

IRREGULAR CUTS
ON ENDS – ADD
INTEREST

IRREGULAR
BEVEL CUT

VERTICAL

CLOCK FACE
OFF- CENTER

HORIZONTAL

Illus. 86

Illus. 87

Illus. 88

Illus. 86   Parallel slab clocks.

Illus. 87   An oblique slab clock, with small pieces of birch markers glued to the walnut.

Illus. 88   Birch dowels or rounded screw-hole buttons also make good hour markers.

Illus. 89 A slab mantel clock made of partially dried butternut. The bark was removed before treatment.

Illus. 90 Here is an idea for an easy-to-make contemporary-styled slab clock. The holes serve as hour markers.

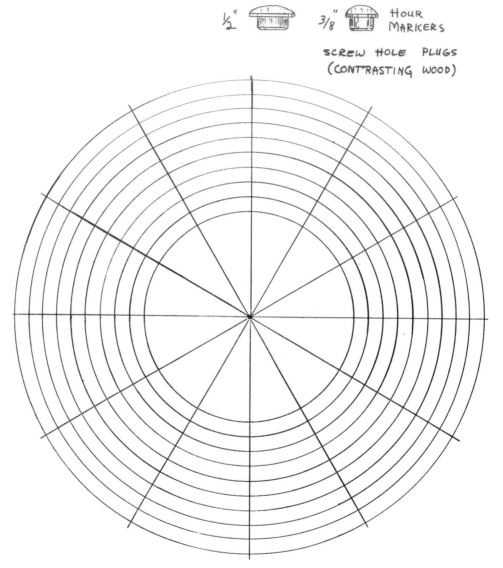

Illus. 91 Pattern for a clock-face templet.

8

Slab Tables

Illus. 92   This rustic table was made from an oblique
slab of 2½-inch-thick butternut. The legs are branches
that were hewed with a draw knife.

$\mathbf{M}$assive slabs make very interesting tabletops. No two of these interesting projects will be the same; each design is dictated by the kind of wood and size of slab you use. Illustrations 92–94 show some of the projects you can make from cross-sectional disks and parallel and oblique-cut log slabs.

Make these tables the same way you would other slab projects. The major problem you will encounter is finding a vat large enough to handle the slabs, legs, and bases that suit your design and supply adequate support.

Level and treat your slab according to the recommendations in the previous chapters. You can treat very large slabs in temporarily devised "one-shot" vats (see Chapter 4). Remember, you can heat these with portable elements to reduce the soaking time. Serious PEG users, those intending to make a good number of large slab tables, may find it more convenient to make a large, shallow vat especially for treating table slabs.

Illus. 94   A cut from a walnut crotch produces this unusually shaped slab table.

Illus. 93   This PEG-treated cross section of a 784-year-old redwood tree measures 38 inches in diameter.

Illus. 95   A king-sized PEG-treated cross section of a large box elder burl.

You can apply PEG to a slab with a brush (Illus. 96). However, when PEG is applied in this way, it will not penetrate the wood as deeply as it will during a soaking treatment and the long-run results will not be as good. Still, it's better to brush-apply PEG than not to apply it at all. Chances for successful treatment with a brush-on application are much better with low-density woods, such as cottonwood, pine, willow, and butternut.

Since the brush-on application will not provide the depth of penetration you get with a complete immersion, it is essential that you remove a minimum of outer shell after treatment and drying. So, before you apply the PEG, work the green wood as close as possible to its final thickness—down to within ⅛ inch (3.2 mm.) of the final size. Normally, you'll have to shave only ⅟₁₆ inch (1.6 mm.) off treated surfaces to remove the extractives, minerals, and pigments that darken the outer layer.

To begin, heat a 50-percent PEG solution in a vat or nonmetallic container to 140 degrees F. (60 degrees C.). Then brush on the solution, completely flooding the surfaces. Slabs with bark attached will soak up good quantities. Repeat this process every other day for three, four, or five weeks, depending upon the species and thickness of the slab.

In order to reclaim drippings and maintain some degree of neatness in the operation, perform the brush-on application over large sheets of heavy-duty polyethylene plastic film. Immediately after applying a coat, wrap the wood in the plastic. This creates a humid environment; without it, the wood will dry out and the brush-on application will not be as effective as it could be.

Remember, the brush-on system is not as predictable as soaking. But the technique often produces good results, and will minimize splitting and checking. Wood treated this way should also retain its bark. Refer to Chapter 12 for information about smoothing and finishing.

You'll find some more ideas for slab tables in Illustrations 97–102.

Illus. 96 These butternut slabs are receiving a brush-on application of a 50-percent PEG solution heated to 140 degrees F. in the vat. Plastic sheeting protects the floor.

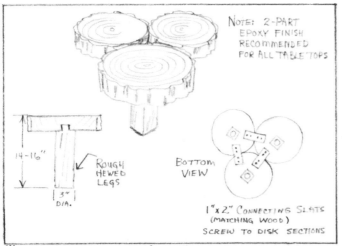

NOTE: 2-PART EPOXY FINISH RECOMMENDED FOR ALL TABLE TOPS

14-16"

3" DIA.

ROUGH HEWED LEGS

BOTTOM VIEW

1"x 2" CONNECTING SLATS (MATCHING WOOD) SCREW TO DISK SECTIONS

GROUT

END GRAIN MOASICS

NOTE: GLUE SLABS TO W/PROOF PLYWOOD BASE WITH EPOXY RESIN, GROUT, SAND, FINISH WITH 2-PART EPOXY

Illus. 97-98   Tabletops of small cross-sectional slabs.

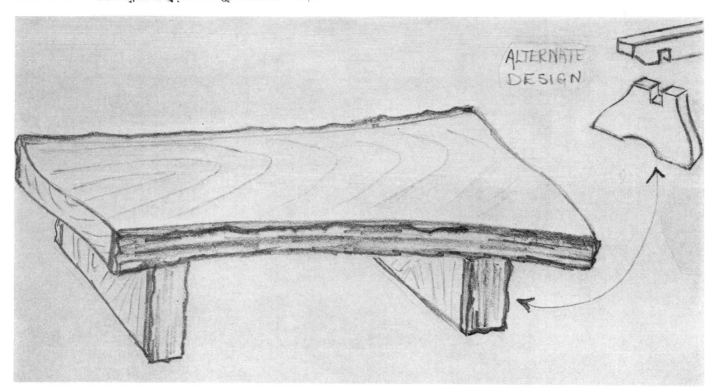

ALTERNATE DESIGN

Illus. 99   A table made from a horizontal slab on vertical slabs.

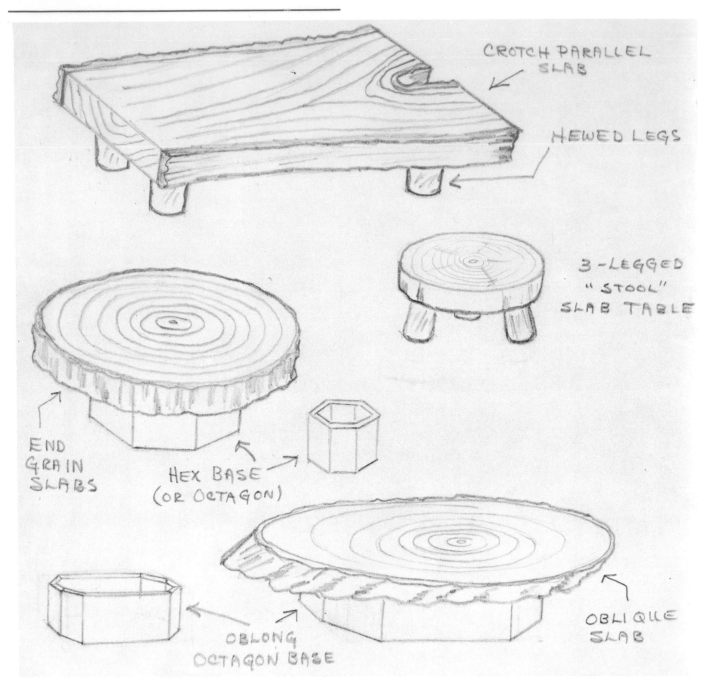

CROTCH PARALLEL SLAB

HEWED LEGS

3-LEGGED "STOOL" SLAB TABLE

END GRAIN SLABS

HEX BASE (OR OCTAGON)

OBLONG OCTAGON BASE

OBLIQUE SLAB

Illus. 100   Large slab coffee tables and some ideas for legs and bases.

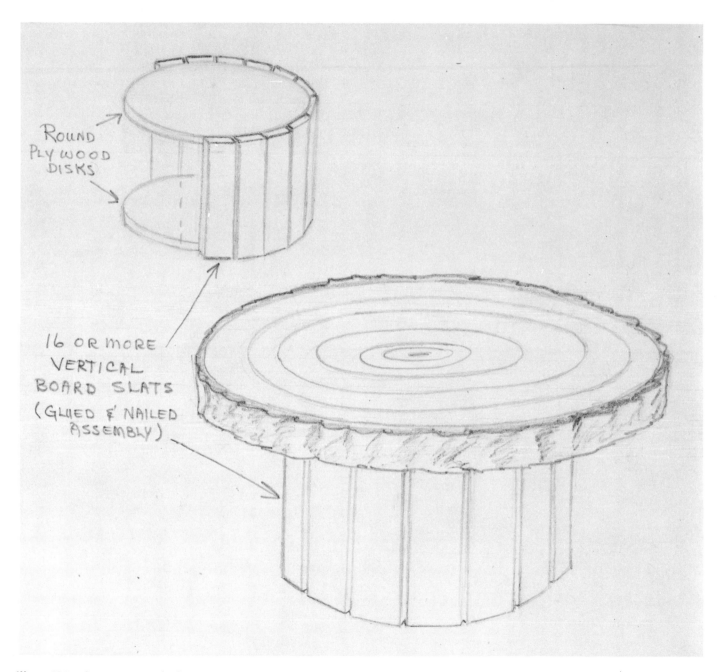

Round
Plywood
Disks

16 or more
Vertical
Board Slats
(Glued & Nailed
Assembly)

Illus. 101   An easy-to-make base system.

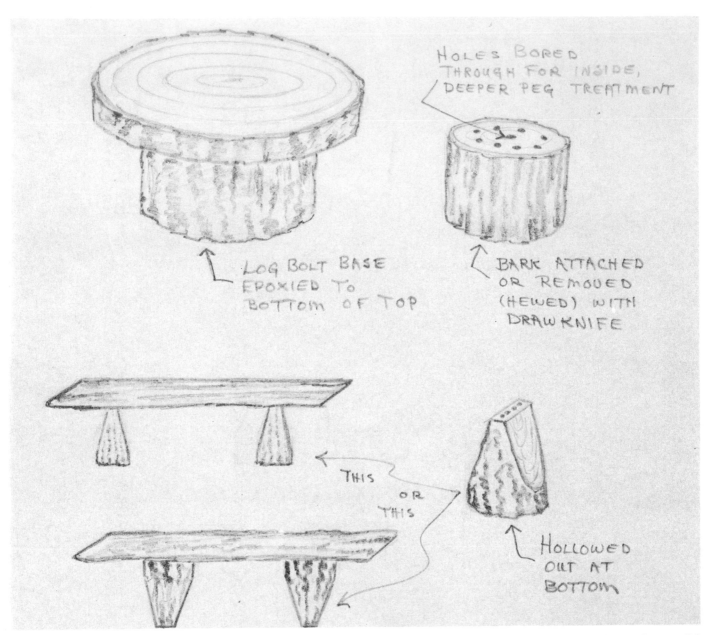

Illus. 102   You can make table bases and legs from solid
log bolts. Drill holes and hollow out areas for PEG
penetration. Attach them with a paste made from mixing
epoxy resin with fiberglass or cotton fibers.

9

Turning Lamp Bases and Heavy Spindles

Illus. 104

Illus. 103   This butternut lamp base features natural bark texture and smooth, distinctive, wavy graining, which is achieved by cutting across the annual rings at a slight angle.

Illus. 104   A small lamp in elm.

Illus. 105   A large lamp in walnut.

Illus. 105

Massive, solid, one-piece lamp bases that you turn on the lathe are unquestionably beautiful. Since every log has its own unique grain, shape, and size, even when cut from the same tree, each turning is one of a kind. See Illustrations 103–108. If you're so inclined, these turnings can bring you a nice profit. I've sold many PEG-treated lamps for well over $100, and have seen weed pots sell for as much as $90.

You will encounter several serious problems when you turn large chunks of wood. First of all, green wood chunks are much heavier than kiln-dried material of the same size and species. These massive chunks are seldom perfectly round, which makes centering and balancing them in the lathe another major concern. If the work is not properly balanced before you turn on the power, the centrifugal force

Illus. 107   Butternut turned clean and smoothly.

Illus. 106   A lamp of popple wood.

Illus. 108   These lamps are of solid walnut.

may throw it from the lathe. Unbalanced pieces may also cause dangerously excessive vibration and damage your lathe. Use a good size, at least a 12-inch (30.48 cm.) lathe. If your lathe is a smaller, lighter-duty type, be especially cautious. Exercise good judgment; never exceed the limits of your equipment.

Because of their excessive thickness, large turnings require extra long treating times in the PEG solution. In general, plan to triple the times suggested for heavy slabs. When possible, hollow out the bottoms or in some other way reduce the thicknesses of the stock. Lamps, table legs, large weed pots, and similar items will not be any less functional (yet still appear solid) if you drill holes into their bottoms (Illus. 109 and 110). When you are working with lamps and weed pots, you can drill holes clear through the center axis or randomly into the thicker areas on the bottoms. With heavy, dense woods, you'll have to drill more holes, and place them closer together, than you will when you work with lighter, less dense, soft woods.

These holes serve two purposes. First, since they

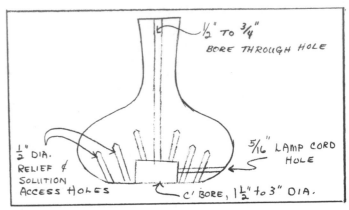

Illus. 110 For massive projects, you should drill holes to relieve stresses and permit deeper PEG penetration.

relieve the natural stresses in the wood that build up during drying, they control and limit cracking and splitting. Second, when you drill holes you expose more areas to treatment, so you get deeper penetration.

You are pushing the performance of the PEG process to the limit by treating these huge, thick pieces. You may have to settle for a little less than a 100 percent success ratio until you have completed several large turnings of the same general size and in the same species. I am experiencing about a 95 percent success ratio without cracks, working in both hard and soft woods, and an overall 100 percent success rate working with butternut and walnut. I am somewhat less successful with denser woods, such as birch and cherry. However, when I weigh the investment of inexpensive or free material, the cost of some PEG, and a little time against the potential rewards, it's certainly worth the effort.

PREPARING THE WORK FOR THE LATHE

Usually, you will find that your tree section is curved along its length and oval in its cross section,

Illus. 109 After this large weed pot of dense locust was rough turned, holes were bored into the bottom. Then it was treated in the PEG solution, dried, and finish turned.

and has branch stubs or similar qualities that will throw the work out of balance when it is mounted in the lathe. It is also likely that the ends you cut with your chain saw are not at exact right angles to the center axis of the log.

Illustrations 111 and 112 show an easily made jig for squaring the ends with a router. Illustration 113 shows a close-up of the routering operation. Make the cut with a regular-width, straight-cutting bit. This system is also good for trueing the ends of log sections you want to use as bases or legs for slab tabletops.

To reduce the possibility of vibration, the router can be used to bring the chunk into balance before it is mounted in the lathe. Illustration 114 shows a jig that is ideal for removing lumps of all sorts. Note that it is adjustable and will accommodate logs of various lengths. A nail driven into the estimated center at each end serves as a pivot point or center. A second nail tacked into the log through one end of the jig holds it steady during routing. Notice the finished piece in Illustration 115. You can also remove lumps with draw knives, chisels, hatchets, chain saws, portable power planes, or band saws, just as long as you get a reasonably balanced piece of wood.

MOUNTING THE WORK IN THE LATHE

The spur center on your lathe may not drive heavy turnings properly. Instead of turning the wood, it may drill a hole in the end. This is especially likely to happen when you start to turn heavy green cylinders of softwoods; and remember, all green wood has weaker fibers than that of dried wood in the same species.

There are ways to guard against this problem. If you square the ends to the axis of the work, you can mount a faceplate to one end. Use as many long,

Illus. 111   This jig, for use with the router set-up in the picture, will easily true the ends of poorly cut logs.

Illus. 112   The log is wedged at the bottom and against the top frame to hold it in its truest vertical position for leveling the first end.

73

Illus. 113   When both end-grain surfaces are completely level, they will be parallel to each other.

Illus. 114   With a router and jig set-up, you can remove "lumps" to balance the log.

heavy-gauge screws as possible. Don't forget to support the other end as usual with the tail stock center. You can also use a special drive center, like the one in Illustration 116, to handle heavy turnings. To make this, you will have to sacrifice a regular spur or dead center that fits your headstock spindle. The drive center in Illustration 116 is made of ¼-inch (3.2 mm.) by 1½-inch (3.8 cm.) by 4-inch (10.16 cm.) steel bar. You can change the size to accommodate your needs or to suit the available material.

Starting the Lathe

Be careful. Always rotate the work by hand before turning on the power. With a visual check,

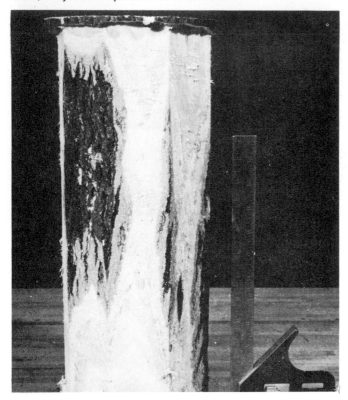

Illus. 115   This once-curved log section is now a balanced piece with trued ends.

Illus. 116   A specially made drive center for turning large cylinders.

make certain that it is properly balanced. Set your lathe to the slowest possible speed. Turn the power on and then quickly turn it off. This way, the work will start coasting down before it reaches its full R.P.M. This technique allows you to determine (for the last and final time) just how well the work "rides" in the lathe. If all appears well, proceed.

I will not debate the merits of the various turning techniques. Professional wood turners make a shearing, cutting action with a gouge and skew, peeling off long, continuous ribbons of dust-free shavings. Others use a flat round nose or a gouge with a scraping action. The objective is to turn the cylinder to a rough, slightly oversized shape that gives you the design profile of your own choice and artistry. Once you have turned your heavy spindle to its rough shape (about ¼ inch [3.2 mm.] oversize), remove it from the lathe. Now drill the holes. Drill lamps straight through on the center axis. If you have a drill press, it will help to start the hole in a truly vertical direction. Complete the hole with a portable power drill, a hand brace, or another similar tool. Incidentally, auger bits do not always cut holes easily into end grains of green softwoods. You can extend a twist drill by welding on a length of drill rod. This works fairly well when driven with hand-held electric drills. Be very careful using long bits in drill presses; if they are not properly balanced or used carefully, they may whip. (Use slow drill-press speeds.) Illustration 110, page 72, shows the typical boring requirements for lamp cords and PEG-access holes.

Immerse the turning in the PEG solution for the recommended time. For added security, you might want to leave it in for a little longer. Remove the work and dry it (see Chapter 6 for more information about drying). When the outer surfaces are thoroughly dry, the work is ready for finish turning, sanding, and finishing. If you have bored holes through the center, you'll have to plug them before you remount the work on the lathe. Glue in hardwood dowels 3 to 4 inches (7.62 cm. to 10.16 cm.) in length with tapered diameters. You can wedge-force these into each end of the turning (Illus. 117).

Illus. 117 When you are preparing a lamp base, drive short, round-tapered plugs into the through hole so you can easily remount it on the lathe for finish turning. Note the PEG-access holes and white plug at the left. The through hole is vividly off center, apparently because the bit followed the grain.

Finish Turning

Mount the work carefully. Be sure it is centered the same way it was for rough turning. Take off only a minimal amount of stock. If you cut too deeply, you will remove the treated, outer shell and you will be turning green wood again. Remember that PEG only penetrates into the outer shell about ¼ to ½ inch (3.2 to 6.4 mm.). After you clean up the surfaces, you can begin sanding. Refer to Chapter 12, pages 105–106, for more information about lathe sanding.

After sanding, drill out the plugs and apply your choice of finish. See Chapter 12 for details on finishing. You might want to apply a good coat of moisture-cure urethane (or better yet, epoxy) to the bottom, end-grain surfaces of heavy turnings. After wiring the lamp, glue on a piece of heavy felt to protect table and other surfaces.

See Illustrations 119–125 for more lamp-base and weed-pot designs. You can combine any of these to create your own designs. Learn to work with the wood; allow the shape and size of the tree, along with the grain features, to shape your design. You'll be pleased with the results.

Illus. 119   Design ideas for spindle turnings.

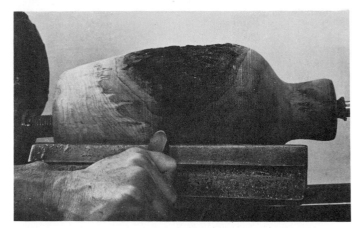

Illus. 118   Finish turning a cherry lamp base. The bark was retained as a design feature.

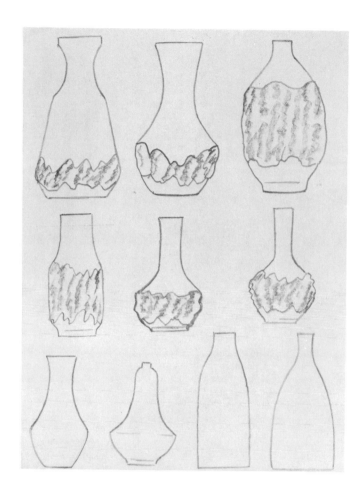

Illus. 121

Illus. 120   Profile shapes for making weed pots. Lamp bases are usually from 15 to 24 inches high. Weed pots are usually much smaller.

Illus. 121   Notice the vivid grain of the butternut.

Illus. 122   A small lamp of locust, only 8 inches high and 6 inches in diameter.

Illus. 122

Illus. 123

Illus. 124

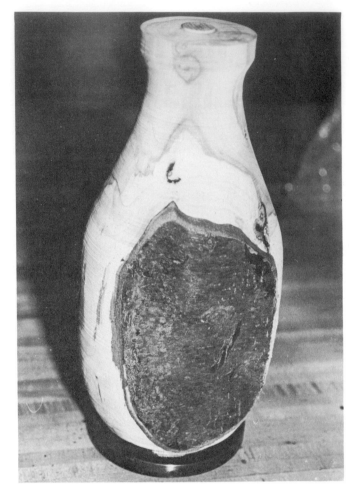

Illus. 125

Illus. 123   This lamp base was made of partially dried butternut.

Illus. 124   This shape exposes the grain pattern.

Illus. 125   This lamp base will have a patch of bark.

10

Making PEG-Treated Wood Bowls

Illus. 126-127   PEG-treated bowls turned directly from green logs.

Making a bowl out of a single piece of PEG-treated wood is an intriguing experience (Illus. 126–130). Beautiful patterns and swirling designs pop out of a common, dirty, and unglamorous log before your eyes. There is only one limitation: the size of the bowl you can make is contingent upon the size of the material available and the capacity of your turning lathe.

You must first determine the best way to turn the log in relation to the tree's growth rings. Should you turn it on its pith center (Illus. 131) or on an axis at right angles to the pith center (Illus. 132)? Should you utilize the crotch area (Illus. 133) or the stump (Illus. 134)? You'll soon learn that you can use almost any part of the tree. Each part will lend its particular qualities to your design.

Because of the stabilizing effect of PEG treatment, you can turn bowls in any position (in relation to the annual rings) without fear of eventual cracking or distortion (warpage) caused by drying. There are few restrictions on the type of wood you can use for bowls. Just be sure it is green, solid, and comes from a species that reacts well to PEG treatment. Remember that PEG will not penetrate areas that have dense, thick knots. When the bowl is thoroughly dry, small checks and fine cracks will develop in these areas.

Since bowls are relatively thin, it is easier—and faster—to treat wood for these projects than it is to treat slabs for tables or the large, bulky pieces you turn into lamp bases. As with other PEG-treated projects, dense, heavy woods and most burls are difficult to treat for bowl turning.

Bowls turned on their pith centers will take the best PEG treatment. This is due to their high percentage of end grain, which PEG penetrates faster and deeper than it does side grain. However, when

Illus. 128   A collection of bowls made at the Forest Products Laboratory as early PEG experiments.

Illus. 129   A butternut bowl turned on its pith center produces lively graining on the slightly curved surfaces.

Illus. 130   This bowl of red oak, turned on its pith center, shows an interesting interplay of light sapwood at the upper area and darker heartwood below.

Chapter 10

Illus. 131-134   Trees into bowls: the drawings show the parts of trees that become the bowls shown in the photos.

Illus. 131

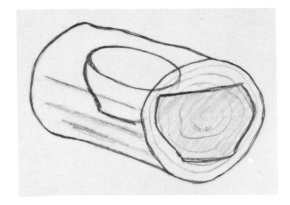

Illus. 132

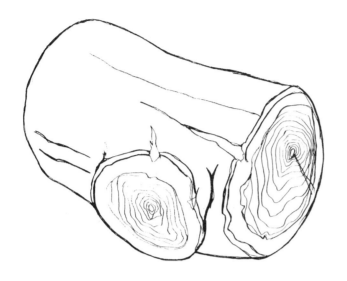

Illus. 133

Illus. 134

you turn a bowl on its center, you'll spend more time severing the end-grain fibers to shape the bowl and sanding.

Since each species of wood has unique qualities, experiment with the woods in your area to determine the proper solution concentration, temperature, and soaking time. Use the information here as a general guideline.

Bowls made from walnut, soft maple, American elm, red oak, cherry, ash, poplar, apple, koa, mango, myrtle wood, white pine, butternut, and similar green woods will all take satisfactory treatment. You can treat most of these with a three-week soak in a 30-percent PEG solution at 73 degrees F. (23 degrees C.)—provided the wall dimension does not exceed ½-inch to ⅝-inch (12.7 mm. to 15.8 mm.) rough-turned thickness. You can treat bowls of this density and size in a much shorter time, from two days to one week, in a 50-percent PEG solution heated to 140 degrees F. (60 degrees C.). I have successfully treated thin-wall butternut bowls with just an over-night soak in a 50-percent solution at 140 degrees F.

You should cut rough bolts for turning bowls as true and round as possible so they will be well balanced on the lathe. Start by chain sawing or band sawing the corners. To make the top and bottom surfaces as parallel as possible, you can use the same router jig you use to parallel the ends of log bolts (see page 73).

MOUNTING THE WORK IN THE LATHE

Before turning on the lathe, make certain that the rough chunk is as evenly balanced as possible. Heavy, unbalanced stock revolving on the lathe is very hazardous. It is always a good idea to ram the tail stock against the free end of the work (Illus. 135) until the outside is turned true (Illus. 136). Remember that screws do not hold well in end grains. When

Illus. 135 A log bolt faceplate mounted and ready for turning on the pith center.

Illus. 136 Trueing the outside.

attaching the faceplate to end-grain surfaces, use long screws of a heavy gauge. Check the screws periodically during turning to be sure they are tight.

Be very cautious when you are working with long, deep turnings of small diameters, such as goblets, mugs, and flowerpots (Illus. 137). Be especially careful when you cut into end grains.

Rough turn the bowls before you place them in the treatment vat. Take them down to no less than ¼ inch (6.3 mm.) of the final thickness and shape. A rough-size wall thickness of ⅜ to ½ inch (9.5 to 12.7 mm.) is even better. Leaving this thickness on rough turnings allows some leeway for recentering the bowl back onto the faceplate after treatment and drying. Also, since the PEG will accumulate on this outer layer and will be removed when you finish cut the bowl, the surface will be clean when you sand and finish the final product. Bases or bowl bottoms can be thicker; about ¾ inch is preferred.

See Illustrations 138–144 for suggestions on preparing a tree-crotch section for mounting on the lathe. It will later be turned into a bowl.

Follow the same steps when you are mounting a bowl that you will turn at a right angle to the pith center. Illustrations 145–150 show the basic steps involved in turning the bowl to a rough size ready for soaking in the vat.

You can air-dry treated bowls in a heated room in three to four weeks. If convenient, hang them by a string from a ceiling rafter to allow air to circulate freely around them. Bowls, like other projects, can also be dried under more severe conditions, such as in a kitchen oven, for six to ten hours at 150 to 180 degrees F. (66 to 82 degrees C.) (see pages 51–52). When the outer shell is sufficiently dry, remount the bowl on the lathe. Make light finish cuts to work it to the final shape and size; you shouldn't have to remove more than ⅛ inch (3.2 mm.) to clean up the surfaces. This operation will remove the stains and waxy accumulation of PEG from the surfaces. Sand the bowl on the lathe with wet-dry sandpaper and finish as desired. See Chapter 12 for more information about sanding and finishing PEG-treated wood. There are more designs in Illustrations 151–155.

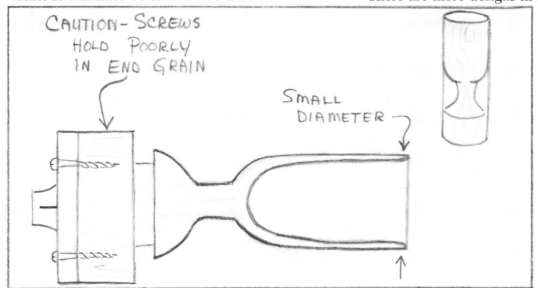

Illus. 137 Since screws do not hold well in end grains, check them periodically when you are turning the work.

Illus. 138

Illus. 139

Illus. 140

Illus. 141

Illus. 143

Illus. 142

Illus. 138   Step 1: Start with a suitable-sized crotch bolt of green wood.

Illus. 139   Step 2: Rough-saw it to an approximately round shape.

Illus. 140   Step 3: Make the surfaces as flat and parallel to each other as possible.

Illus. 141   Step 4: Level the second surface, making it parallel to the opposite surface.

Illus. 142   Step 5: Lay out the major diameter.

Illus. 143   Step 6: If a band saw is available, saw the bolt to a round shape. Otherwise, remove lumps with a chain saw, router, or other hand tools.

Illus. 144   Step 7: Attach the faceplate.

Illus. 144

Illus. 145   This log bolt will be turned on a center axis perpendicular to the growth rings. A faceplate will be attached and the bolt will be lathe mounted.

Illus. 146   The bolt is mounted in the lathe and is ready for initial rough turning. Note that the tail stock center is rammed against the work for added support.

Illus. 147   Trueing the outside brings the work into balance and the preliminary profile shape begins to evolve. The lines of the grain often indicate the optimum shape.

Illus. 148   After finalizing the outside shape, true the open end before moving the tail stock center away.

Illus. 149   Hollow out the inside. Work to a wall thickness not exceeding ½ inch.

Illus. 150   The completed rough-turned bowl. Remove the faceplate and place the bowl into the vat for PEG treatment.

Illus. 151   A nut bowl in walnut.

Illus. 152   A small bowl in soft maple.

Illus. 153

Illus. 155

Illus. 153   A wood cup of soft maple holds kitchen utensils.

Illus. 154   A small bowl in ash.

Illus. 155   Some profile shapes for bowls.

Illus. 154

11

Miscellaneous Projects and Processes

Illus. 156   Planter and vases of green walnut.

There are more turning projects, such as weed pots, bud vases, planters, and candle holders, in Illustrations 156–166. You can band saw single, flat, curved surfaces to produce some very interesting projects. The clocks in Illustration 167 and the lamp in Illustration 168 are typical examples. The essential problem with this type of work, as with carvings, is that the surfaces are difficult to smooth and sand. You have to do most of the finish work by hand. You'll soon learn it takes lots of elbow grease to obtain smoothly finished surfaces. Smooth out saw marks and other irregularities with Stanley "Surform"® tools; these clog less than regular wood files or rasps.

COMPOUND BAND SAWING PROJECT SHAPES

Compound band sawing is a technique that allows you to make four-sided projects with irregular curved cuts. You make these cuts on a pattern laid out on two adjoining surfaces of a squared bolt (Illus. 169). This technique allows you to make four-sided lamp bases, weed pots, candle holders, massive table bases, carving blanks, and many other projects from log bolts (Illus. 170). In fact, you can convert most of the round-turning projects in this book into four-sided projects.

SEASONING GREEN WOOD CARVINGS

Treat carvings like you would any other project. As always, work the piece to as near the final shape as possible before treatment (Illus. 171 and 172). When you are not working on the project, immerse it in water or wrap it in sheet plastic to maintain its green condition. You can hollow out or drill holes into the bottom of any carving with a massive base (Illus. 173–175). This relieves the natural stresses in the wood, minimizes the tendency to split, and more

importantly, permits penetration of PEG into a high-hazard area from both outside and inside.

Since most carvings will be fairly thick, treat them about twice as long as you would bowls. Air-dry them, add the final surface details, then sand and finish them according to any of the procedures in Chapter 12.

If a carving is too large to treat by immersion, melt some PEG and brush it on the surface. Then wrap the carving in plastic film to maintain the humidity; this facilitates the diffusion of the PEG into the wood. Repeat this operation about four times at one-week intervals. Remove the plastic and air-dry the carving, then proceed with the usual final details and finishing. Although this technique is not as surefire as immersion soaking, it often produces good results and will minimize checking.

Illus. 157 This rustic planter is a branch length, the inside of which has been bored out.

Illus. 158

Illus. 159

Illus. 160

Illus. 161

Illus. 158   The high percentage of end grain in this vase allowed for good treatability.

Illus. 159   Bark-attached locust weed pots.

Illus. 160   Small bud vases.

Illus. 161   A butternut chalice.

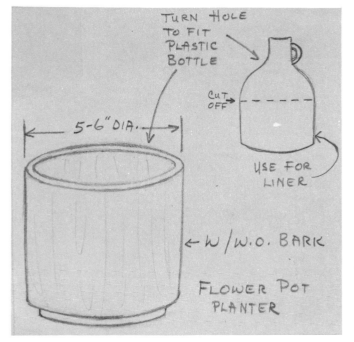

Illus. 163

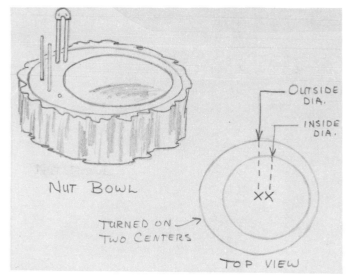

Illus. 162   Another design for a bud vase.

Illus. 163   An idea for making a planter.

Illus. 164   An idea for making a nut bowl.

Illus. 164

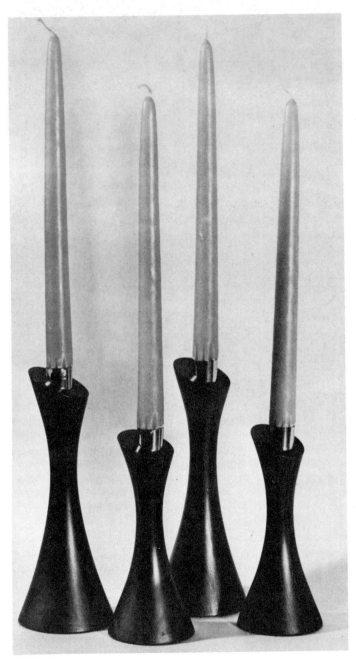

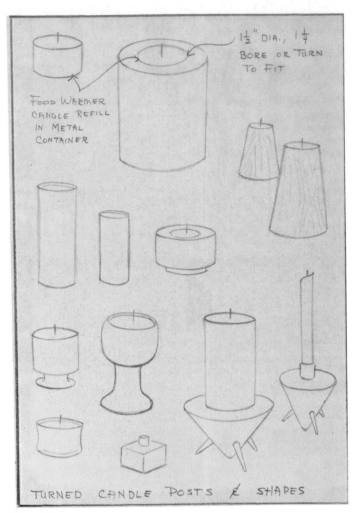

Illus. 166

Illus. 165   You can make slim candle holders like these from small branches.

Illus. 166   Ideas for candle holders.

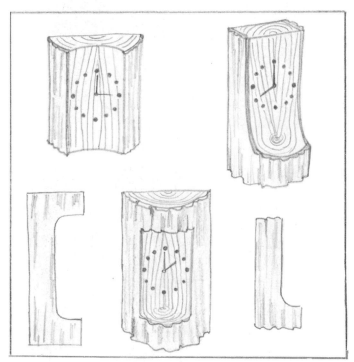

Illus. 167

Illus. 169

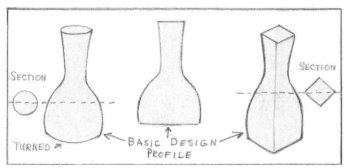

Illus. 168

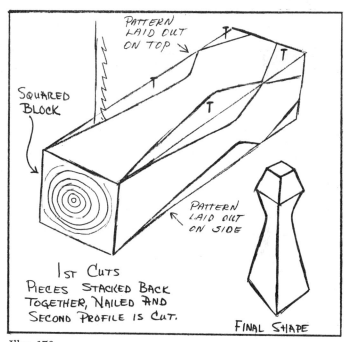

Illus. 170

Illus. 167   Some clock ideas.

Illus. 168   You can turn this basic design profile to a **round** shape or band-saw it to a square shape.

Illus. 169   A log bolt with one band-saw cut makes this unusual lamp base.

Illus. 170   Four-sided shapes made by compound band sawing.

Illus. 171-172   Green wood carvings can be treated effectively with PEG.

Illus. 173

Illus. 175

Illus. 174

Illus. 173   A carving of
PEG-treated green cherry
wood.

Illus. 174   A hand-carved
owl in white cedar.

Illus. 175   In this decorative decoy, the pith center
runs at an angle through
the bill, angling downward
through the lower neck.

Illus. 176   A hand-carved owl from a tree crotch. Notice the heavy, intricately carved base.

PROTECTING IMPORTED CARVINGS

Woodcarvers in tropical countries almost always use partially dried wood. When these carvings are brought into the United States and exposed to our rather low humidities, they will crack and split. Many carvings are ruined after only one or two weeks in our air-conditioned and heated buildings.

At the first sign of checking or splitting, immerse the carvings in water until you can treat them. If the cracks swell shut, you can be certain that the PEG treatment will be completely successful. If, however, the cracks do not close completely when you immerse the wood in water, they will remain open even after the PEG treatment. PEG will only prevent further damage.

Remember that it is better to overtreat than to undertreat woods. Carvings of extremely dense, tropical hardwoods are difficult to treat at ambient temperatures; you may have to increase the solution temperature to 100 degrees F. (38 degrees C.) or more.

After treating the carvings, air-dry them for about three to six weeks (depending on size and shape), preferably in a heated room. Water-soaking and PEG-treatment will remove most of the shoe polish or cheap varnish with which many of these carvings are finished. Remove the remainder by sanding. Then bleach, sand, and refinish them with the finish suggested for bowls and green-wood carvings.

If you treat the carvings as soon as you purchase them, they will be fully protected against future checking and splitting.

GLUEING PEG-TREATED WOOD

Although many common glues, including the popular white glue (a polyvinyl), do not work well on PEG-treated wood, several widely available, high-quality glues do work well. Among them are two-component waterproof resorcinol and epoxy glues of various brands. The hobbyist's standby, the urea-resin type, also works well, but it is not quite as resistant to water.

For best results, use a good PEG solvent on the wood surface just before the glue is applied; this will cut the wax and expose the fibers. For critical joints that require maximum structural strength, as in laminated gun stock blanks, scrub the surface with a toluol soaked cloth. When it has dried, wash it again with wood alcohol. Then apply the glue. You can omit the toluol step on less critical joints.

PEG-TREATED WOOD FOR EXTERIOR USE

PEG-stabilized disks are sometimes used to pave outdoor patios (Illus. 177 and 178) and to make rustic projects that will ultimately be in contact with moist soil. You must protect these disks against

Illus. 177   Patio disks and bench legs (the ones pictured are made of split tree crotches) can be PEG treated.

Illus. 178   After you treat patio disks with water-repellent preservative, lay them on a base of sand, topped with 1 inch of pea gravel. Fill in between the disks with more gravel.

101

attack by insects, such as termites, and decay organisms. Since PEG is soluble in water, it will eventually leach out of unprotected, treated disks exposed to rains. For the best protection against insects, decay, and leaching, apply a good water-repellent preservative stain that contains a wax to shed water and an active insecticide-fungicide such as pentachlorophenol. Good water-repellent preservative stains are available at most paint stores. The more wax and pigment you use in the formulation, the better the performance will be under adverse conditions.

Apply several coats of the water-repellent pre-outdoor use, you should consider using a species of servative to the wood before installing it in an outdoor exposure, and add one coat each year. For outdoor use, you should consider using a species of wood with high, natural resistance to insects and decay, such as redwood, cedar, or cypress. When possible, cut away the outer band of sapwood, which is less resistant to decay, before treating the wood with PEG.

12

Smoothing and Finishing

Illus. 179

104

People will ultimately judge any handcrafted project by the quality of its finish. In this chapter, you will find the basic information you need to finish a PEG-treated project professionally. Remember, however, that each manufacturer supplies instructions for his own brand of finish; since I can only supply general information, be sure to follow the manufacturer's instructions carefully.

SMOOTHING AND SANDING

You will quickly discover that PEG-treated wood reacts to smoothing and sanding differently than untreated wood. First, knife-cut the surfaces as closely as possible using the jointer, turning chisel, hand plane, carving knife, or whatever tool is most appropriate. As you already know, PEG-treated wood cuts cleaner and easier with edge tools than untreated wood. Stanley "Surform" tools work very well on three-dimensional or irregularly curved surfaces.

Sand in the direction of the grain, as you would untreated wood. Begin your sanding with 80-, 100-, or 120-grit abrasive, depending on the surface condition of your wood. Regular (garnet) abrasives (Illus. 180) will quickly load up with PEG; medium and fine grits will load up especially fast. For best results, use coarse grits. These won't leave deep, hard-to-remove scratches.

"Wet-or-dry" sandpapers (Illus. 181 and 182) are especially effective on PEG-treated wood. Water, which is a solvent for PEG, will dissolve waxy sawdust from these papers (Illus. 183). In fact, you can even use water as a lubricant for the sanding opera-

Illus. 179   Most finishes effectively hold water in (or out, as shown), but the best finish is one that will form a barrier to resist the passage of vapor.

tion. It is a good idea to use two pieces of paper for each step. Soak one piece in warm water (dissolving the waxy sawdust) while you use the other piece.

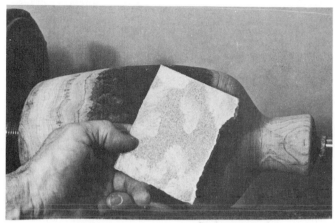
Illus. 180   When you dry-sand PEG-treated wood, regular abrasives will quickly load up with waxy sawdust.

Illus. 181   Wet-or-dry waterproof sandpapers are recommended for PEG-treated wood.

Illus. 182   Lathe-work sanding is clean and easy with wet-or-dry abrasives.

Illus. 183   This waxy sawdust will dissolve quickly with warm water.

Don't use water if you sand with an electric sander (Illus. 184)—you could get a shock. Air-driven sanders are ideal for power wet sanding. Use a wire brush to clean clogged abrasives (Illus. 185). If hard-to-remove accumulations develop on the

sandpaper, remove the belt or sheet from the sander and soak it in hot water.

BLEACHING

Sometimes the outer ⅟₁₆ inch (1.6 mm.) of your wood will darken during treatment. This condition is caused by the concentrated pigments, minerals, and extractives that develop during long and high-temperature treatments. You can remove these darkened surfaces by bleaching with oxalic acid. Dissolve 4 heaping tablespoons of oxalic

Illus. 184   Power dry-sanding a flat surface.

acid crystals (obtainable at most drug stores) in 1 cup of hot water. Apply the solution liberally with a rag (Illus. 186) or brush. Oxalic acid is a poison, so handle it carefully. Wear rubber gloves and be careful to keep the solution out of your eyes.

After you have let your bleaching solution soak in for an hour or so, remove the excess acid by sponging the surface with a rag dampened in a dilute solution of household ammonia. Allow the wood to dry for a day, then sand it with fine grit wet-or-dry

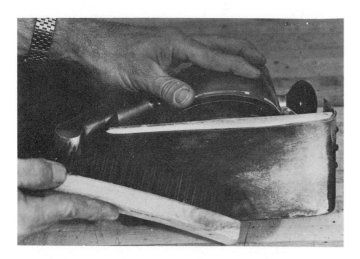

Illus. 185   Use a wire brush to clean clogged sandpaper.

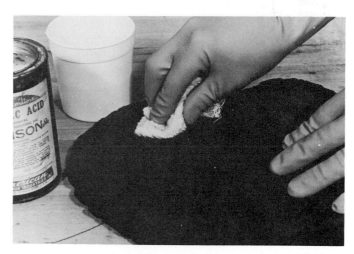

Illus. 186   Applying bleach with a rag.

paper to remove any raised grain or scratches. Again, allow the wood to dry thoroughly, then apply one of these finishes: special moisture-cure and regular polyurethane varnish, penetrating natural Danish oil, or epoxy. Most conventional wood finishes, such as lacquers, do not work well on PEG-treated wood.

MOISTURE-CURE AND REGULAR POLYURETHANE VARNISHES

You should use moisture-cure varnish as a base coat over heavily PEG-treated wood, as well as on those projects with a high degree of exposed end-grain surfaces. This type of finish will set up rapidly on a wet surface or when it is exposed to atmospheric moisture, is extremely hard and durable, and most important, is quite effective in sealing PEG in the wood during prolonged periods of high humidity. It is thick and sticky and tends to leave brush marks. Work it quickly. Sand the surface thoroughly between coats, using 220-grit or finer paper.

Apply up to four or five coats of the moisture-cure varnish at full strength (without thinning) at one-day intervals. For best results, follow this treatment up with one, two, or more coats of any good grade of conventional (chemically hardened) polyurethane varnish—the type commonly available at paint stores for furniture and house trim. It may take as long as two days for the first coat of regular polyurethane to set up. However, subsequent coats will harden in 12 hours or less. Polish with pumice or rubbing compound, which is available from automotive parts stores. Be careful not to cut through the final coat of the regular polyurethane varnish. Buff and polish with paste wax.

USING REGULAR POLYURETHANE VARNISHES

You won't need to apply a base coat of moisture-cure polyurethane to projects that are relatively easy to finish. Examples are lightly treated carvings, bowls, and other projects that have a minimum of end-grain surfaces, are not made from oblique-cut slabs, and are not likely to be exposed to extremely high humidities for prolonged periods of time. For these projects, use conventional polyurethane varnishes. They are easy to apply by brush or spray, they adhere well to treated wood, and are fairly hard and durable. Generally, for the first coat, it is a good idea to dilute the regular polyurethane resin varnish with an equal amount of mineral spirits or turpentine. Use this mixture as a sealer. Allow it to dry, sand lightly with 220-grit paper, and apply subsequent coats at full strength. Lightly sand or steel wool between coats as usual, and follow up the treatment with a coat of paste wax.

DANISH OIL FINISH

Of the many oil-type "natural" finishes, the Danish oil penetrating finish performs most satisfactorily on PEG-treated wood, especially on indoor projects having a lot of exposed end grain. This finish is very easy to apply. Danish oil is good for almost all projects, including those that are likely to be exposed to periods of high humidities. However, when you apply Danish oil to heavily PEG-treated surfaces, they may become tacky, especially during humid periods.

Danish oil finish does not produce a gloss or satin sheen, as do the film-forming polyurethanes and epoxies. It has a beautiful, rich, raw-looking appearance that highlights natural grains extremely well. Danish oil is intended to penetrate deeply into the wood and, by chemical reaction with the natural wood substances, harden or cure within the wood itself. One of its major advantages is that it is so easy to apply. In addition, you won't run into the problems, such as brush marks, air bubbles, or dust buildup, that you encounter with polyurethanes and epoxies.

To apply Danish oil, flood the surfaces, allowing the finish to penetrate deeply within the wood. Normally, this takes about forty-five minutes to an hour. Sand the surface when it is still wet with a fine,

Illus. 187   Applying Danish oil finish. Step 1: Flood the surface.

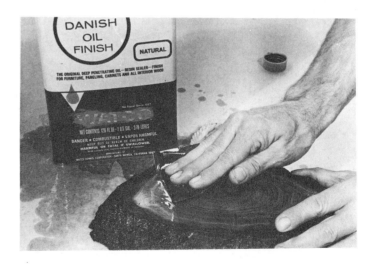

Illus. 188   Step 2: After you flood the surface and allow the oil to penetrate deeply, sand with fine grit while the surface is still wet with oil.

Illus. 189 Step 3: Wipe all surfaces, removing excess oil with a dry, absorbent rag.

wet or dry abrasive, using the oil as a lubricant. Wipe off all of the excess finish with a dry, absorbent rag. Excess finish remaining on the surface will become sticky; be sure you wipe it all off.

You can apply Danish oil finish in dusty shops without worry, and you can handle the project immediately after the final wiping without leaving fingerprints. If after a day or so the surface appears to be a little oil-starved, just give it more oil, wet-sand it, and wipe it dry. Danish oil is ideal for bark-attached projects; the spongelike bark accepts the penetrating Danish oil exceptionally well. See page 113 for more specific instructions about finishing bark-attached projects.

Epoxies are the most serviceable film-forming finishes for PEG-treated wood. Their major advantage is their percentage of solids, which are excellent moisture barriers. Other finishes, such as lacquers, urethanes, and polyesters, hold water out (or in) but they contain solvents and other flowing agents that

evaporate during drying. As they evaporate, they leave small microscopic openings in the finish, allowing water vapor to pass through and settle on the wood.

There are hundreds of different epoxy formulations. To finish PEG-treated wood, use the heavy-bodied, single-application, flow-on polymer epoxy finishes or those with a thin consistency and good penetrating and adherence qualities. You will get deeper penetration and better adherence with epoxies of thinner viscosities, but you will have to apply several coats to get a suitable film depth. On the other hand, flow-on polymer epoxies are easy to apply. Particularly on flat-level surfaces, you'll only need to apply one coat.

Since epoxies have toxic effects on some people, heed all warnings the manufacturer provides. It is always a good idea to wear disposable plastic gloves.

Mix the appropriate amounts of accurately measured resin and hardeners (Illus. 190) in a clean container, such as a nonwaxed paper cup or reusable plastic bowl. Mix thoroughly (Illus. 191) and apply as directed. When you are applying flow-on epoxies to flat surfaces (Illus. 192), such as clock slabs and tabletops, the surface must be as level as possible if you are to achieve a uniform film thickness. Elevate the project on scrap blocks to enable the excess to run off freely. Pour the epoxy on the surface and spread it with a clean, stiff paper trowel, such as an index card (Illus. 193). Use a brush to coat the edges (Illus. 194).

The flow-on epoxies have exceptional self-leveling qualities, so you should keep troweling and brushing to a minimum. If air bubbles get trapped under the coating of varnish, blow lightly on the surface or pass a propane torch over it from a distance of 6 to 10 inches (15.24 to 25.4 cm.) (Illus.

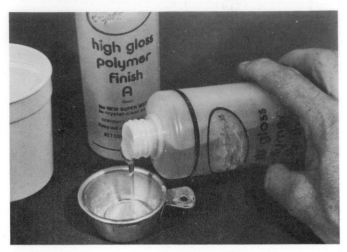

Illus. 190   Applying flow-on epoxy finish. Step 1: Accurately measure the appropriate amount of resin and hardeners.

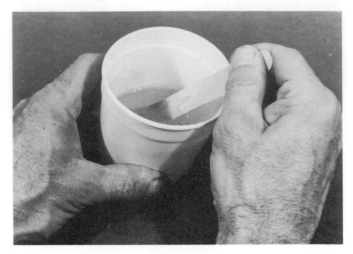

Illus. 191   Step 2: Mix thoroughly.

Illus. 192   Step 3: Pour on.

Illus. 193   Step 4: Spread with clean, stiff paper to pull the finish over uncoated areas.

Illus. 194   Step 5: Dab the epoxy into bark crevices with a brush.

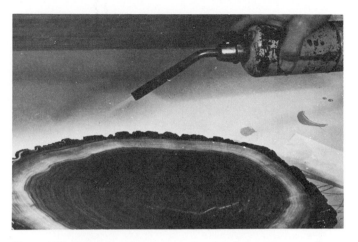

Illus. 195   Step 6: Use a propane torch to remove air bubbles created during mixing.

Illus. 196   Step 7: Protect the work with an appropriate dustcover, such as a clean piece of cardboard or a clean box.

195). If the bubbles still don't pop, puncture them with a pin. Always cover freshly epoxied surfaces with a dust cover (Illus. 196).

Depending upon the absorbent qualities of the wood, the finish should be complete with one application. However, if the finish penetrates too deeply, or if you spread it too thin, you can apply another coat, usually without any surface preparation. When you are flow-on finishing plaques, clocks, tabletops, and similar items, the run-off over the edges forms undesirable drips. You must remove these by filing or sanding after curing. To alleviate this problem altogether, prepare the bottom with paste wax or Vaseline before you finish the piece (Illus. 197). Since the epoxy drippings won't adhere to wax or Vaseline you can remove them easily. Clean up brushes and tools with acetone or epoxy solvent.

You can cut the super high-gloss of epoxies to a beautiful, rich satin finish. Simply sand the piece lightly with 500- or 600-grit paper, and then apply rubbing compound and paste wax.

Illus. 197   By applying paste wax to the bottom surface perimeter before you finish the work, you will make drip removal easier.

Illus. 198   Sanding through to the raw wood is likely to cause a "blotchy" finish.

You will have no trouble using flow-on epoxies on three-dimensional projects, such as carvings and turnings, unless you intend to rub down the finish to remove the gravity sags or brush marks. Since the finish pulls thin on the upper areas or protrusions, it is very easy to cut through to the raw wood in these areas (Illus. 198). You are likely to get a blotched finish, even if you apply a second coating.

If you have applied the epoxy correctly, you can add other finishes. You must be sure, however, that the epoxy buildup is sufficient. It is a good idea to touch-sand the epoxy-finished surface before you apply another kind of finish over it. You might want to make a test piece to check out the compatibility and adhesion quality of the finish with the epoxy base.

An extra finish over the epoxy base *does not* offer more protection for locking in PEG and moisture. However, the advantages of an extra finish are that it eliminates a lot of hand rubbing and sanding you would have to do to "spruce up" a coat of epoxy and permits you to use finishes that do not adhere directly to PEG-treated wood. For example, there are two ways to cut the high gloss of epoxy: you can either hand rub the piece, or simply apply a coat of satin lacquer finish, such as Deft®. While Deft won't adhere directly to PEG-treated wood, it will adhere to wood treated with epoxy (Illus. 199 and 200).

Here is an effective finishing system for PEG-treated projects (this technique does not apply to bowls you will be eating from):

1   Finish with penetrating Danish oil; allow to cure for three days to one week.

2   Apply epoxy over the oil finish. Use flow-on epoxies for flat, horizontal surfaces. Use thinner-consistency epoxies with brush-on application for turnings. Sometimes you will need as many as five coats to get a suitable film depth.

3   Spray on lacquers or brush on Deft or a similar material as the final finish (this step is optional).

Illus. 199　One of several brush-on applications of an epoxy base coat. Note the extremely high gloss.

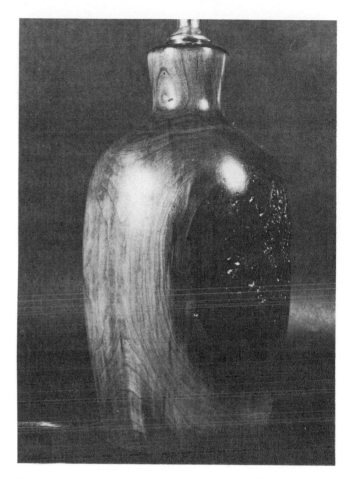

Illus. 200　The super gloss of epoxy has been softened to a satin sheen by a lacquer-type finish.

FINISHING BARK-ATTACHED PROJECTS

Bark is very porous and absorbs greater quantities of PEG than wood does. During prolonged periods of high humidities, the PEG in the bark (PEG is hygroscopic) sops up so much atmospheric moisture that the bark becomes water soaked, ruining any built-up polyurethane varnish finishes. For the most natural-looking and serviceable bark finish, use Danish oil.

Danish oil penetrates deeply into the porous structure, does not form a continuous surface film, and will withstand high humidities. If you want a polyurethane-varnish or epoxy finish on a tabletop or other bark-attached slab project, apply a coat of Danish oil first. Then apply the varnish or epoxy to the flat surface of the top, including the sanded edge of the thin ribbon of bark around the circumference. Be careful—don't allow the epoxy finish or varnish

113

to run over the edge onto the rough surfaces of the oil-finished bark.

You can apply the epoxy or varnish to the entire project, not just the top. However, projects that have been flooded like this usually don't look as natural and epoxy gives a "plastic" look to the bark.

You can finish decorative wood bowls like you would any other PEG-treated wood. If you are going to eat out of them, finish the insides with olive oil, corn oil, or any other vegetable oil. Peanut oil makes an especially good finish since it will not turn rancid. If you decide to use a commercial finish, check with the manufacturer regarding its safety.

Appendix

Distributors of Polyethylene Glycol-1000 (PEG)

Bulk

Crane Creek Company
Dow Corning Corporation
McKesson Chemical Company
Union Carbide Corporation

Retailers

Robert M. Albrecht
Constantine & Son, Inc.
Craftsman Wood Service Co.
Crane Creek Company
Industrial Arts Supply Company
Lee Valley Tool
Lemont Specialties
PITSCO, Inc.
Spielmans Wood Works
Wilken-Anderson Company
Woodcraft Supply Corp.

Distributors of Equipment and Other Supplies

PEG Vats

Crane Creek Company
IASCO
PITSCO
Spielmans Wood Works

Vat Heating Elements

Spielmans Wood Works

Portable Heating Elements

Spielmans Wood Works

Mini-Vaps (evaporation barrier)

Spielmans Wood Works

Polyurethane Varnish (moisture cure)

Crane Creek Company

Epoxy Finishes

Craftsman Wood Service
Crane Creek Company
Gougeon Brothers, Inc.

Danish Oil Finishes

Constantine & Son, Inc.
Craftsman Wood Service
Crane Creek Company
IASCO
The Upholstery Supply Co.
Woodcraft Supply Corp.
The Woodworkers Store

Hydrometers

Crane Creek Company
Spielmans Wood Works

Laboratory Ovens

IASCO
PITSCO

Clock Movements

Constantine & Son, Inc.
Craftsman Wood Service
Crane Creek Company
National Artcraft Supply Co.
Woodcraft Supply Corp.
The Woodworkers Store

Distributors of Equipment (Cont.)

LAMP PARTS
Constantine & Son, Inc.
Craftsman Wood Service
Gearon Co.
National Artcraft Supply Co.
W. N. deSherbimin Products, Inc.
Woodcraft Supply Corp.
The Woodworkers Store

FELT
Constantine & Son, Inc.
Craftsman Wood Service

Woodcraft Supply Corp.
The Woodworkers Store

FLUSH MOUNTING WALL HANGERS
Woodcraft Supply Corp.
The Woodworkers Store

BRASS FERRULES (CANDLE SOCKETS)
Constantine & Son, Inc.
Craftsman Wood Service
The Upholstery Supply Co.
The Woodworkers Store

Companies and Suppliers—Addresses

Albrecht
8635 Yolanda Avenue
Northridge, CA 91324

Atlas West Corp.
20 Jericho Turnpike
Jericho, NY 11753

The Brookstone Co.
127 Vose Farm Road
Peterborough, NH 03458

Coastal Abrasive and Tool Co.
1 Nutmeg Drive
Trumbull, CT 06611

Conover Woodcraft Specialties, Inc.
18124 Madison Road
Parkman, OH 44080

Constantine & Son, Inc.
2050 Eastchester Road
Bronx, NY 10461

Craft Products Co.
North Avenue and Route 83
Elmhurst, IL 60126

Craftsman Wood Service Co.
2727 South Mary Street
Chicago, IL 60608

Crane Creek Company
P.O. Box 5553
Madison, WI 53705

Creative Craft Plans
739 Sprague Road
Indianapolis, IN 46217

Curtis Woodcraft Supply Co.
344 Grandview Street
Memphis, TN 38111

Dow Corning Corp.
P.O. Box 1592
Midland, MI 48640

Frank Mittermeier, Inc.
East Tremont Avenue
Bronx, NY 10465

Frank Paxton Lumber Co.
6311 St. John Avenue
Kansas City, MO 64123

Frog Tool Co. Ltd.
541 North Franklin Street
Chicago, IL 60610

Companies and Suppliers (Cont.)

Garrett Wade Co. Inc.
302 5th Avenue
New York, NY 10001

Gatson Wood Finishes
Dept. NC
P.O. Box 1246
3630 East 10th Street
Bloomington, IN 47401

Gearon Co.
3225 West 26th Street
Chicago, IL 60623

General Woodcraft
100 Blinman Street
New London, CT 06320

Goldblatt Tool Co.
559–U Osage
Kansas City, KS 66110

Gougeon Brothers, Inc.
706 Martin Street
Bay City, MI 48706

IASCO (Industrial Arts Supply Co.)
5724 West 36th Street
Minneapolis, MN 55416

The Japan Woodworker
1004 Central Avenue
Alameda, CA 94501

John Harra Wood and Supply Co.
39 West 19th Street
New York, NY 10011

Lee Valley Tools
857 Boyd Avenue
Ottawa, Ontario
Canada K2A 2C9

Leichtung, Inc.
701 Beta Drive, Number 17
Cleveland, OH 44143

Lemont Specialties
Box 271
Lemont, PA 16851

Love-Built Toys and Crafts
2907 Lake Forest Road
P.O. Box 5459
Tahoe City, CA 95730

McKesson Chemical Co.
2955 Packers Avenue
Madison, WI 53704

Masonry Specialty Co.
172 Westbrook Road
New Kensington, PA 15068

Merritt Abrasive Products Inc.
201 West Manville
Compton, CA 90224

National Artcraft Supply Co.
23456 Mercantile Road
Beachwood, OH 44122

Newport Enterprises, Inc.
2309 West Burbank Boulevard
Burbank, CA 91506

PITSCO, Inc.
P.O. Box 1328
Pittsburg, KS 66762

Shopsmith, Inc.
750 Center Drive
Vandalia, OH 45377

Spielmans Wood Works
188 Gibraltar Road
Fish Creek, WI 54212

Union Carbide Corp.
270 Park Avenue
New York, NY 10017

U.S. General Supply Co.
100 General Place
Jericho, NY 11753

The Upholstery Supply Co.
12530 West Burleigh Road
Brookfield, WI 53005

Wilkens-Anderson Co.
4525 West Division Street
Chicago, IL 61651

Wood Carvers Supply Co.
3056 Excelsior Boulevard
Minneapolis, MN 55416.

Woodcraft Supply Corp.
313 Montvale Avenue
Woburn, MA 01801

The Woodworkers Store
21801 Industrial Boulevard
Rogers, MN 55374

Metric Conversions

Approximate Conversions to Metric Measures

Symbol	Multiply	by	To Find	Symbol	Symbol	Multiply	by	To Find	Symbol
								Volume	
Length					tsp	teaspoons	5	milliliters	ml
in	inches	*2.5	centimeters	cm	Tbsp	tablespoons	15	milliliters	ml
ft	feet	30	centimeters	cm	fl oz	fluid ounces	30	milliliters	ml
yd	yards	0.9	meters	m	c	cups	0.24	liters	l
					pt	pints	0.47	liters	l
Area					qt	quarts	0.95	liters	l
in²	square inches	6.5	square cm.	cm²	gal	gallons	3.8	liters	l
ft²	square feet	0.09	square meters	m²	ft³	cubic feet	0.03	cubic meters	m³
yd²	square yards	0.8	square meters	m²	yd³	cubic yards	0.76	cubic meters	m³
Mass (weight)					*Temperature (exact)*				
oz	ounces	28	grams	g					
lb	pounds	0.45	kilograms	kg	°F	Fahrenheit temperature	5/9 (after subtracting 32)	Celsius temperature	°C

Approximate Conversions from Metric Measures

Symbol	Multiply	by	To Find	Symbol	Symbol	Multiply	by	To Find	Symbol
								Volume	
Length					ml	milliliters	0.03	fluid ounces	fl oz
mm	millimeters	0.04	inches	in	l	liters	2.1	pints	pt
cm	centimeters	0.4	inches	in	l	liters	1.06	quarts	qt
m	meters	3.3	feet	ft	l	liters	0.26	gallons	gal
m	meters	1.1	yards	yd	m³	cubic meters	35	cubic feet	ft³
					m³	cubic meters	1.3	cubic yards	yd³
Area					*Temperature (exact)*				
cm²	square centimeters	0.16	square inches	in²					
m²	square meters	1.2	square yards	yd²	°C	Celsius temperature	9/5 (then add 32)	Fahrenheit temperature	°F
Mass (weight)									
g	grams	0.035	ounces	oz					
kg	kilograms	2.2	pounds	lb					

*1 inch = 2.54 cm (exactly)

Measuring Equivalents and Formulas

1 gallon	=	4 quarts
1 quart	=	2 pints
		4 cups
		946.4 milliliters
1 pint	=	2 cups
		16 fluid ounces
1 cup	=	16 tablespoons
		8 fluid ounces
		236.6 milliliters
1 tablespoon	=	3 teaspoons
		½ fluid ounce
		14.8 milliliters
1 teaspoon	=	4.9 milliliters
1 liter	=	1000 milliliters
		1.06 quarts
1 U.S. gallon	=	231 cu. in.
1 gallon	=	231 cu. in.
1 cu. ft.	=	7.48 gal.

1 cu. ft. water	=	62.425 lbs. (max. density)
1 gallon water	=	8.337 lbs.
1 liter	=	.264178 gallon (U.S.)
Cubic feet	=	gallons × 0.1337

Specific gravity = number of times a substance is as heavy as an equal body of water, or Specific gravity (liquid) =

$$\frac{\text{weight of liquid}}{\text{weight of equal volume of water}}$$

Specific gravity (solid) =

$$\frac{\text{weight of body}}{\text{weight of equal volume of water}}$$

or Specific gravity (solid) =

$$\frac{\text{weight of body}}{\text{loss of weight in water}}$$

$$\text{Density} = \frac{\text{weight}}{\text{volume}}$$

Perimeter		Area		Volume	
scalene ▲	$P = a + b + c$	rectangle	$A - lw$	cylinder	$V = Bh$
isosceles ▲	$P = 2a + b$	square	$A = lw$ or $A = s^2$	rectangular solid	$V = lwh$
equilateral ▲	$P = 3s$	parallelogram	$A = bh$	cube	$V = e^3$
quadrilateral	$P = a + b + c + d$	triangle	$A = \frac{1}{2}bh$	circular cylinder	$V = \pi r^2 h$
rectangle	$P = 2l + 2w$	trapezoid	$A = \frac{1}{2}h\,(b_1 + b_2)$	pyramid	$V = \frac{1}{3}Bh$
square	$P = 4s$	circle	$A = \pi r^2$	cone	$V = \frac{1}{3}Bh$ or $\frac{1}{3}\pi r^2 h$
circle	$C = \pi d$ or $C = 2\pi r$	cube	$A = 6e^2$	sphere	$V = \frac{4}{3}\pi r^3$ or $\frac{4\pi r^3}{3}$

P=perimeter	b=base (length)
C=circumference	b=area of base
A=area	h=height (length)
V=Volume	e=edge (length)
w=width	π=3.14 or $\frac{22}{7}$
l=length	

Scalene ▲ has all sides of unequal length
Isosceles ▲ has two sides of equal length
Equilateral ▲ has all sides of equal length
Quadrilateral is any four-sided figure

Index